SLOW COOKER curries

hamlyn

SLOW COOKER curries

Over **150** delicious recipes with intense flavour

Sunil Vijayakar

An Hachette UK Company
www.hachette.co.uk

First published in Great Britain in 2010 by
Hamlyn, a division of Octopus Publishing Group Ltd
Endeavour House
189 Shaftesbury Avenue
London
WC2H 8JY
www.octopusbooks.co.uk

ISBN 978-0-600-62154-6

A CIP catalogue record for this book
is available from the British Library

Printed and bound in China

10 9 8 7 6 5 4 3 2

Contents

Introduction

The word 'curry' is thought to derive from the South Indian Tamil word *kari*. It's generally used to describe any spiced, saucy dish, best known in the cuisines of India, Sri Lanka, Bangladesh, Indonesia, Malaysia, Burma (Myanmar), Thailand and other South Asian and Southeast Asian countries. Today we now know and love a wide variety of curries that come from different places around the world. They differ greatly in their taste and content, with vast regional variations and originating from many well-defined cuisines, each with its own history.

If you're a curry lover, then no doubt you'll have tried to emulate a certain delicious recipe you had at a restaurant, or a sumptuous dish you experienced on holiday, only to find that your home-cooked curry lacks that certain something. It's difficult to define what makes a good curry – is it depth and intensity of flavour, or tenderness of ingredients? All good curries require attention to an essential blend of herbs and spices, and a slow release of spectacular flavours. That's where your trusty slow cooker comes in.

This book contains over 150 recipes for curries that you can cook in a slow cooker. From Creamy Lamb Korma (page 20) and Cambodian Pork & Lemon Grass Curry (page 48) to Balinese Mango & Chicken Curry (page 60), Tobago Crayfish Curry (page 148) and Filipino Green Papaya Curry (page 168), you'll discover how slow cooking can bring fantastic curries from all around the world to life. With such a huge selection of recipes, including over 40 recipes for rice and pulse dishes, plus creative twists on classic accompaniments such as Jamaican Fresh Peach Chutney (page 246) and Burmese Cucumber Pickle (page 250), you'll be spoilt for choice.

A perfect match

Slow cookers are back in vogue and are now being used to prepare all manner of meals – not just a meaty stew or a chicken pot roast. In fact, slow cookers emulate ancient cooking techniques from all around the world, where blending ingredients requires patience, care and a creative mind, which means that they are a fantastic cooking tool for curries. Slow cooking spices allows them to release their essential oils, while meat becomes beautifully tender and vegetables absorb tasty hotness, zing and zest.

What's more, a slow cooker will make life easier, saving you time and money in the kitchen. Slow cooked curries can be a simple treat on any day of the week and needn't be a last-minute thought on a Friday night before calling for a takeaway.

Spending as little as 15–20 minutes early in the day is all that's needed to prepare supper to go into a slow cooker, leaving you free to get on with something else. Because the food cooks so slowly there's no need to worry about it boiling dry, spilling over or burning on the bottom, and (depending on the setting) it can be left for 8-10 hours.

A slow cooker is environmentally friendly, too. There's no need to turn on the oven for just one dish when you can save fuel by using your slow cooker. It uses around the same amount of electricity as an electric light bulb, so is cheap to run. In addition, the long, slow cooking transforms even the toughest and cheapest cuts of meat into dishes that melt in the mouth, and the meat literally falls off the bone.

Finding a curry that's right for you

The most common misconception is that a curry is a hot and spicy dish. Of course, some curries are extremely hot, but on the whole most recipes are a balanced blend of spices and herbs with a delicate and sophisticated flavour. This book offers exciting recipes to suit every palate. Follow the simple chilli guide at the side of the recipes to see whether a curry is hot or mild. There are over 150 recipes from all over the world– opening your mind to a plethora of cooking styles and flavours that you probably never knew existed. Why not try Moroccan Spiced Vegetable Tagine (page 156) or Tamarind Fish Curry (page 138) for a particularly mild flavour or the Beef Madras (page 54) or Thai Green Chicken Curry (page 76) if you're a chilli fan.

Whatever its origins, a curry usually contains a selection of fresh and dried herbs and spices. (In the recipes, these are assumed to be fresh unless otherwise stated.) Depending on the dish, other ingredients could include chillies, curry leaves, ginger, garlic, shallots, lemon grass, coconut milk, palm sugar, tamarind paste, Thai fish sauce, shrimp paste and chopped tomatoes – the list goes on. The recipes and ingredients vary from region to region, as well as from country to country.

You can buy most of the ingredients in any large supermarket, and with the miracle of internet shopping you can even order exotic ingredients and have them delivered to your door.

Slow cooker know-how

Size matters

Slow cookers are available in three sizes and are measured in capacity. The size usually printed on the packaging is the working capacity or the maximum space for food:

- For two people, use a small oval slow cooker with a maximum capacity of 1.5 litres (2½ pints) and a working capacity of 1 litre (1¾ pints).
- For four people, choose a medium-sized round cooker or the more versatile oval cooker with a total capacity of 3.5 litres (6 pints) and a working capacity of 2.5 litres (4 pints).
- For six people, you'll need a large oval slow cooker with a total capacity of 5 litres (8¾ pints) and a working capacity of 4 litres (7 pints) or the extra large round 6.5 litres (11½ pints) with a working capacity of 4.5 litres (8 pints).

Surprisingly, the very large slow cookers cost only a little more than the medium-sized ones, and it's easy to be swept along thinking that they are better value for money. However, unless you have a large family or like to cook large quantities so that you have enough supper for one meal with extra portions to freeze, you'll probably find that they're too big for your everyday needs. Remember that you need to half-fill a slow cooker when you're cooking meat, fish or vegetable dishes. The best and most versatile shape for a slow cooker is an oval, which is ideal for cooking a whole chicken and has ample room for a pudding basin or four individual pudding moulds and yet is capacious enough to make soup for six portions. Choose one with an indicator light so that you can see at a glance when the slow cooker is turned on.

Before you start

It's important to read the handbook before using your slow cooker. Some manufacturers recommend preheating the slow cooker on the high setting for a minimum of 20 minutes before food is added. Others recommend that the it's is heated only when filled with food. A slow cooker pot must only be used with the addition of liquid – ideally it should be no less than half full. Aim for the three-quarter full mark, or make sure the liquid is no higher than 2.5 cm (1 inch) from the top.

Heat settings

All slow cookers have 'high', 'low' and 'off' settings, and some also have 'medium', 'warm' or 'auto' settings. Both settings will reach just below 100°C (212°F), boiling point, during cooking, but when the cooker is set to 'high' the temperature is reached more quickly. A combination of settings can be useful and is recommended by some manufacturers at the beginning of cooking. See your manufacturer's handbook for more details.

Timings

All the recipes in the book have variable timings, which means that they will be tender and ready to eat at the lower time, but can be left without spoiling for an extra hour or two, which is perfect if you get delayed at work or stuck in traffic. If you want to speed up or slow down the cooking process based on diced meat or vegetables so that the cooking fits around your plans better, adjust the heat settings and timings as suggested below:

Low	Medium	High
6–8 hours	4–6 hours	3–4 hours
8–10 hours	6–8 hours	5–6 hours
10–12 hours	8–10 hours	7–8 hours

(The above timings were taken from the Morphy Richards slow cooker instruction manual. Note: don't change timings or settings for fish, whole joints or dairy dishes.)

Using a slow cooker for the first time

Before you start to use the slow cooker, put it on the work surface, somewhere out of the way, and make sure that the flex is tucked around the back of the machine and not trailing over the front of the work surface.

The outside of the slow cooker does get hot, so warn young members of the family, and don't forget to wear oven gloves or use tea towels when you're lifting the pot out of the housing. Set it on a heatproof mat on the table or work surface when you're ready to serve the food.

If your slow cooker lid has a vent in the top, make sure that the slow cooker is not put under an eye-level cupboard or the steam may catch someone's arm as they reach into the cupboard.

Always check that the joint, pudding basin, soufflé dish or individual moulds will fit into your slow cooker pot before you begin work on a recipe, to avoid frustration when you get to a critical point.

Preparing food for the slow cooker

MEAT Cut meat into pieces that are the same size so that cooking is even, and fry off meat before adding to the slow cooker. Check it's cooked either

by using a meat thermometer or by inserting a skewer through the thickest part and checking that the juices run clear.

VEGETABLES Root vegetables can (surprisingly) take longer to cook than meat. If you're adding vegetables to a meat casserole, make sure you cut them into pieces that are a little smaller than the meat, and try to keep all the vegetable chunks the same size so that they cook evenly. Press the vegetables and the meat below the surface of the liquid before cooking begins.

FISH AND SHELLFISH If the fish or shellfish was frozen it must be thoroughly thawed, rinsed with cold water and drained before use. Whether you cut fish into pieces or cook it in a larger piece of about 500 g (1 lb), the slow, gentle cooking will not cause it to break up or overcook. Make sure that the fish is covered by the hot liquid so that it cooks evenly right through to the centre. Don't add shellfish until the last 15 minutes of cooking, and make sure that the slow cooker is set to high.

RICE Easy-cook rice is preferable for slow cookers because it has been partially cooked during

manufacture and some of the starch has been washed off, making it less sticky. Allow a minimum of 250 ml (8 fl oz) water for each 100 g (3½ oz) easy-cook rice, and up to 500 ml (17 fl oz) water for 100 g (3½ oz) risotto rice.

DRIED PULSES Make sure that you soak dried pulses in plenty of cold water overnight. Drain them, then put them in a saucepan with fresh water and bring to the boil. Boil rapidly for 10 minutes, then drain or add with the cooking liquid to the slow cooker. See the recipes for details. Pearl barley and lentils (red, Puy or green) don't need soaking overnight. If you're unsure, check the instructions on the packet.

CREAM AND MILK Cream and milk are not generally added at the beginning of cooking, except when you're making rice pudding or baked egg custard-style dishes. Use full-fat milk

where milk is cooked directly in the cooker pot rather than pudding moulds, as it's less likely to separate.

Changing recipes to suit a different model

All the recipes in this book have been tested in a medium-sized, four-portion slow cooker (see details on page 8). However, you might have a small, two-portion cooker or a large, six-portion cooker. To adapt the recipes in this book, simply halve the amounts for two portions, or add half as much again for six portions, keeping the timings the same.

Caring for your slow cooker

If you look after it carefully, you may find that your machine lasts for 20 years or more. Because the heat of a slow cooker is so controllable, it's not like a saucepan with burned-on grime to contend with. Simply lift the slow cooker pot out of the housing,

fill it with hot soapy water and leave it to soak for a while. It's tempting to pop the slow cooker pot and lid into the dishwasher, but they do take up a lot of space, and you should always check with your manufacturer's handbook first, because not all are dishwasher-proof.

Allow the machine itself to cool down before cleaning. Turn it off at the controls and pull out the plug. Wipe the inside with a damp dishcloth, removing any stubborn marks with a little cream cleaner. The outside of the machine and the controls can be wiped with a dishcloth, then buffed up with a duster; or, if it has a chrome-effect finish, spray it with a little multi-surface cleaner and polish with a duster.

Never immerse the machine in water to clean it. If you're storing the slow cooker in a cupboard, make sure it's completely cold before you put it away.

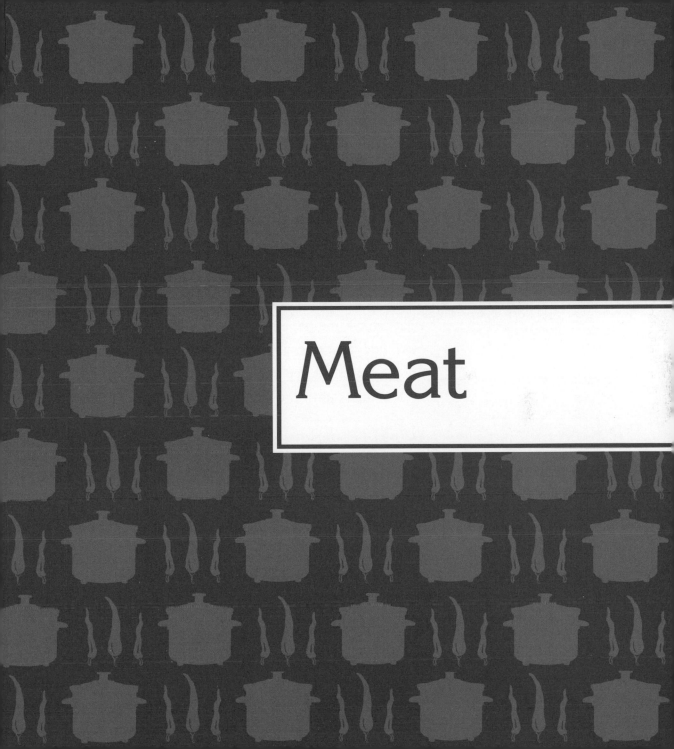

Meat

Preparation time	**20 minutes**
Cooking temperature	**low**
Cooking time	**6¼–8¼ hours**
Serves	**4**
Heat rating	🌶🌶🌶

1 tablespoon **sunflower oil**

1 **onion**, finely chopped

1 teaspoon peeled and finely grated **galangal**

3 tablespoons **Thai red curry paste**

875 g (1¾ lb) thick **pork steaks**, cut into bite-sized pieces

750 ml (1¼ pints) **chicken stock**

25 g (1 oz) finely chopped **coriander** (including root and stem)

2 **lemon grass stalks**, bruised

4 tablespoons **tamarind paste**

1 tablespoon grated **palm sugar**

6 **kaffir lime leaves**

small handful of **Thai sweet basil leaves**

Bangkok sour pork curry

Heat the oil in a large heavy frying pan over a medium heat. Add the onion and fry for 3–4 minutes until soft. Add the galangal, red curry paste and pork, and stir-fry for 4–5 minutes until the meat is well sealed.

Transfer this mixture to the slow cooker pot. Pour over the stock and add the coriander, lemon grass, tamarind, palm sugar and lime leaves. Cover with the lid and cook for 6–8 hours or until the pork is tender.

To serve, transfer the curry to a serving bowl and scatter over the Thai sweet basil leaves just before serving with thick egg noodles.

Preparation time	**15 minutes**
Cooking temperature	**low**
Cooking time	**6¼–8¼ hours**
Serves	4
Heat rating	🌶🌶

Caribbean curried beef

Season the beef with salt and pepper. Heat the oil in a large frying pan over a high heat. Add the beef and brown all over for 5–6 minutes until well sealed.

Add the cloves, onion and curry powder, and sauté for 2–3 minutes until the onions are starting to soften and turn translucent, then stir in the carrots, celery, thyme and garlic. Sauté for a further 2 minutes.

Transfer this mixture to the slow cooker pot. Stir in the tomato purée and pour over the beef stock to just cover the meat. Stir well, then add the potato and black-eyed beans. Cover with the lid and cook for 6–8 hours or until the meat is tender.

Serve hot with rice.

875 g (1¾ lb) **beef sirloin**, cut into bite-sized pieces

3 tablespoons **vegetable oil**

6 **whole cloves**

1 **onion**, finely chopped

2 tablespoons **curry powder**

2 **carrots**, roughly chopped

2 **celery sticks**, diced

1 tablespoon **thyme leaves**

2 **garlic cloves**, crushed

4 tablespoons **tomato purée**

750 ml (1¼ pints) **beef stock**

1 large **potato**, peeled and diced

200 g (7 oz) **tinned black-eyed beans**, rinsed and drained

salt and **pepper**

Preparation time	20 minutes
Cooking temperature	low
Cooking time	6¼–8¼ hours
Serves	4
Heat rating	🌶🌶

4 tablespoons **sunflower oil**

625 g (1¼ lb) boned **shoulder of lamb**, cut into bite-sized pieces

1 **onion**, finely chopped

3 **garlic cloves**, finely grated

2 teaspoons **ground turmeric**

1 teaspoon **ground ginger**

1 teaspoon **ground cinnamon**

1 teaspoon **paprika**

large pinch of freshly grated **nutmeg**

200 g (7 oz) **golden raisins** or **sultanas**

200 g (7 oz) **dried apricots**

400 g (13 oz) **tinned chopped tomatoes**

300 ml (½ pint) **vegetable** or **lamb stock**

salt and **pepper**

whisked **Greek yogurt**, to drizzle (optional)

Turkish lamb curry
with apricot & sultanas

Heat half the oil in a large heavy saucepan and brown the lamb in batches for 3–4 minutes. Remove with a slotted spoon and set aside.

Heat the remaining oil in the pan and add the onion, garlic, turmeric, ginger, cinnamon, paprika, nutmeg, raisins or sultanas and apricots. Stir-fry for 1–2 minutes until fragrant, then add the lamb. Stir-fry for 2–3 minutes and transfer the mixture to the slow cooker pot.

Add the tomatoes and stock and stir to mix well. Season well with salt and pepper and cover with the lid. Cook for 6–8 hours or until the lamb is very tender.

Serve hot with Turkish pide bread or rice and drizzled with yogurt, if liked.

Preparation time	**15 minutes, plus marinating**
Cooking temperature	**low**
Cooking time	**6¼–8¼ hours**
Serves	**4**
Heat rating	🌶🌶🌶

Pork vindaloo

Put the pork in a non-reactive dish. Rub the paste all over the pork so that it is well mixed, cover with clingfilm and leave to marinate in the refrigerator for up to 24 hours.

Heat the oil in a large heavy saucepan over a medium-high heat. When the oil is hot, add the onion and stir-fry for 3–4 minutes. Add the chilli powder, turmeric, cumin and pork, and stir-fry for a further 3–4 minutes until the meat is well sealed.

Transfer the pork mixture to the slow cooker pot. Stir in the potatoes, tomato purée, sugar, chopped tomatoes and stock. Season well with salt and pepper, and cover with the lid. Cook for 6–8 hours or until the pork is meltingly tender.

Garnish with chopped coriander and serve immediately with steamed white rice.

625g (1¼ lb) boneless **pork tenderloin**, cut into bite-sized pieces

4 tablespoons **vindaloo paste**

2 tablespoons **sunflower oil**

1 **onion**, finely chopped

1 tablespoon **chilli powder**

1 teaspoon **ground turmeric**

2 teaspoons **ground cumin**

4 **potatoes**, peeled and quartered

100 ml (3½ fl oz) **tomato purée**

1 tablespoon **sugar**

400 g (13 oz) **tinned chopped tomatoes**

400 ml (14 fl oz) **chicken stock**

salt and **pepper**

chopped **coriander leaves**, to garnish

Preparation time	**20 minutes, plus soaking**
Cooking temperature	**high**
Cooking time	**2–3 hours**
Serves	4
Heat rating	🌶 🌶

Vietnamese spiced beef & noodle broth

150 g (5 oz) **dried rice noodles**

50 g (2 oz) **bean sprouts**

6 **spring onions**, finely sliced

small handful of **mint leaves**

small handful of **coriander leaves**, roughly chopped

1 **red chilli**, sliced

2 **limes**, cut into wedges

250 g (8 oz) **fillet steak**, very thinly sliced

FOR THE BROTH

900 ml (1½ pints) **beef stock**

6 **whole cloves**

10 **whole black peppercorns**

3 cm (1¼ inch) piece of **root ginger**, peeled and sliced

3 **cinnamon sticks**

3 **star anise**

6 green **cardamom pods**

2 tablespoons **fish sauce** such as nuoc mam, plus extra to serve

To make the broth, pour the stock into the slow cooker pot, add the spices and the fish sauce, and cook for 2–3 hours.

Put the rice noodles in a large bowl, cover well with boiling water and leave to soak for 15 minutes.

Meanwhile, put the bean sprouts, mint and coriander leaves, chilli, lime wedges and some fish sauce in separate small bowls, and arrange them on a large plate.

Divide the sliced fillet steak and rice noodles among 4 warm serving bowls. Ladle the boiling hot stock from the slow cooker over each bowl. Serve immediately, allowing guests to help themselves to the accompaniments.

Preparation time	15 minutes
Cooking temperature	low
Cooking time	6¼–8¼ hours
Serves	4
Heat rating	

2 tablespoons **sunflower oil**

875 g (1¾ lb) **lamb neck fillet**, thinly sliced

2 tablespoons **ghee**

1 **onion**, finely chopped

2 **garlic cloves**, finely chopped

2 teaspoons peeled and finely grated **root ginger**

50 g (2 oz) **ground almonds**

1 tablespoon **white poppy seeds (khus)**

5 tablespoons **korma curry paste**

400 ml (14 fl oz) **lamb stock**

250 ml (8 fl oz) **single cream**

salt and **pepper**

Creamy lamb korma

Heat the oil in a large nonstick frying pan over a medium-high heat, and brown the lamb in batches for 2–3 minutes. Remove with a slotted spoon and set aside.

Add the ghee to the pan and reduce the heat to medium. When the ghee is hot, add the onion, garlic and ginger, and fry for 3–4 minutes until the onion is soft. Stir in the ground almonds, poppy seeds and curry paste, and stir-fry for 1–2 minutes.

Transfer the onion mixture to the slow cooker pot with the reserved lamb. Add the stock and cream. Season with salt and pepper, stir and cover with the lid. Cook for 6–8 hours or until the lamb is very tender, stirring occasionally.

Serve immediately with warm naan breads or parathas.

Preparation time	**10 minutes, plus marinating**
Cooking temperature	**low**
Cooking time	**6¼–8¼ hours**
Serves	4
Heat rating	🌶

Burmese red pork curry

In a small bowl, mix together the soy sauce and tomato purée. Put the pork in a non-reactive dish, pour over the soy mixture and toss to coat evenly. Cover and leave to marinate in the refrigerator for 6–8 hours, or overnight if time permits.

Heat the oil in a heavy saucepan over a medium heat. Add the sugar and stir for a few minutes until the sugar has dissolved and is starting to caramelize. Add the curry powder, garlic and ginger, and stir-fry for 2 minutes.

Add the marinated pork (including any marinade) and stir to mix well. Remove from the heat and transfer into the slow cooker pot. Add just enough water to cover the meat, cover with the lid and cook for 6–8 hours or until the pork is tender and the liquid has almost evaporated.

100 ml (3½ fl oz) **light soy sauce**

100 ml (3½ fl oz) **tomato purée**

875 g (1¾ lb) boneless **pork loin**, cubed

2 tablespoons **groundnut oil**

1 tablespoon **soft brown sugar**

1 tablespoon **curry powder**

2 **garlic cloves**, finely sliced

1 tablespoon peeled and finely grated **root ginger**

Preparation time	**20 minutes, plus marinating**
Cooking temperature	**low**
Cooking time	**6½–8½ hours**
Serves	**4**
Heat rating	

Calcutta beef curry

500 g (1 lb) **stewing beef**, cut into bite-sized pieces

75 ml (3 fl oz) **natural yogurt**

3 tablespoons **hot curry powder**

2 tablespoons **mustard** or **sunflower oil**

1 dried **bay leaf**

1 **cinnamon stick**

3 **whole cloves**

4 **green cardamom pods**, bruised

1 large **onion**, halved and thinly sliced

3 **garlic cloves**, minced

1 teaspoon peeled and finely grated **root ginger**

400 ml (14 fl oz) **beef stock**

¼ teaspoon **garam masala**

salt

Put the beef in a non-reactive bowl. In a small bowl, mix together the yogurt and curry powder, and pour over the meat. Season with salt, cover with clingfilm and leave to marinate in the refrigerator for 24 hours.

Heat the oil in a large frying pan over a medium heat. Add the bay leaf, cinnamon, cloves and cardamom pods, and stir-fry for 1 minute until fragrant. Add the onion and stir-fry for 4—5 minutes, before adding the garlic and ginger. Stir-fry for a further 1 minute.

Reduce the heat to low, add the marinated beef and stir-fry for 10—15 minutes.

Transfer this mixture to the slow cooker pot. Pour over the beef stock. Cover with the lid and cook for 6—8 hours or until the beef is meltingly tender.

Check the seasoning, stir in the garam masala and serve immediately with steamed basmati rice.

Preparation time	**15 minutes**
Cooking temperature	**low**
Cooking time	**6¼–8¼ hours**
Serves	**4**
Heat rating	

Ceylonese black pork curry

2 **onions**, roughly chopped

3 cm (1¼ in) piece of **root ginger**, peeled and roughly chopped

4 **garlic cloves**, roughly chopped

2 tablespoons **vegetable oil**

6 **curry leaves**

1 **cinnamon stick**

8 **cardamom pods**

2 tablespoons **medium curry powder**

875 g (1¾ lb) boneless **pork leg**, cut into large cubes

1 tablespoon **wine vinegar**

1 tablespoon **tamarind paste**

200 ml (7 fl oz) **water**

200 ml (7 fl oz) **coconut cream**

1 **red chilli**, deseeded and finely sliced

salt

Put the onions, ginger and garlic in a food processor, and blend until finely chopped.

Heat the oil in a large frying pan or wok over a medium heat. Add the onion mixture and fry for 2–3 minutes, stirring constantly so that it doesn't burn. Add the curry leaves, cinnamon stick, cardamom pods and curry powder, and stir-fry for 1 minute until fragrant. Add the pork and stir-fry for 6–8 minutes or until well coated with the mixture.

Transfer to the slow cooker pot. Stir in the vinegar, tamarind paste and measurement water, and season with salt. Cover with the lid and cook for 6–8 hours or until the pork is tender.

Stir in the coconut cream and the red chilli just before serving.

Preparation time	**20 minutes**
Cooking temperature	**low**
Cooking time	**6½–8½ hours**
Serves	**4**
Heat rating	

Lamb rogan josh

2 tablespoons **sunflower oil**

625 g (1¼ lb) boneless **lamb shoulder**, cut into large bite-sized pieces

2 large **onions**, halved and thickly sliced

3 **garlic cloves**, minced

2 teaspoons peeled and finely grated **root ginger**

2 **cassia bark** or **cinnamon sticks**

2 teaspoons **Kashmiri chilli powder**

2 teaspoons **paprika**

6 **green cardamom pods**

4 tablespoons **medium curry paste**

400 g (13 oz) **tinned chopped tomatoes**

6 tablespoons **tomato purée**

1 teaspoon **sugar**

600 ml (1 pint) **lamb stock**

4–6 medium **potatoes**, peeled and halved

salt and **pepper**

chopped **coriander leaves**, to garnish

Heat half the oil in a large heavy flameproof casserole over a medium-high heat. Cook the lamb in batches for 3–4 minutes until well sealed and browned. Remove with a slotted spoon and set aside.

Add the remaining oil to the casserole and reduce the heat to medium. When the oil is hot, add the onions and fry for 10–12 minutes, stirring often, until soft and lightly browned.

Add the garlic, ginger, cassia or cinnamon, chilli powder, paprika and cardamom pods. Stir-fry for 1–2 minutes, then add the curry paste and lamb. Stir-fry for 2–3 minutes.

Transfer this mixture to the slow cooker pot. Stir in the tomatoes, tomato purée, sugar, stock and potatoes. Season well with salt and pepper, cover with the lid and cook for 6–8 hours or until the lamb is meltingly tender.

Serve garnished with chopped coriander.

Preparation time	**20 minutes**
Cooking temperature	**low**
Cooking time	**6¼–8¼ hours**
Serves	**4**
Heat rating	♪ ♪ ♪

4 **beef fillet steaks**, about 100 g (3½ oz) each

1 tablespoon **sunflower oil**

2 tablespoons **Thai red curry paste**

400 ml (14 fl oz) **coconut milk**

200 ml (7 fl oz) **beef stock**

2 tablespoons **fish sauce** such as nam pla

1 tablespoon **lime juice**

6 **kaffir lime leaves**, finely shredded

225 g (7½ oz) **tinned bamboo shoots**, rinsed and drained

small handful of **Thai sweet basil leaves**

Thai red beef curry

On a clean work surface, sandwich the steaks between 2 sheets of clingfilm. Using a meat mallet or the side of a rolling pin, pound the steaks until evenly flattened and about 1 cm (½ inch) thick. Cut the beef into thin strips.

Heat the oil in a large heavy saucepan over a medium-high heat. Add the beef in batches and stir-fry for 2–3 minutes until well sealed. Remove with a slotted spoon and transfer to the slow cooker pot.

Add the curry paste, coconut milk, stock, fish sauce, lime juice, kaffir lime leaves and bamboo shoots. Cover with the lid and cook for 6–8 hours or until the meat is tender.

Stir in the basil leaves just before serving hot with steamed jasmine rice.

Preparation time	**15 minutes**
Cooking temperature	**low**
Cooking time	**6–8 hours**
Serves	**4**
Heat rating	

Massaman lamb curry

Put the lamb in the slow cooker pot with the stock, curry paste, tamarind, coconut milk, lemon grass, shallots and butternut squash. Cover with the lid and cook for 6–8 hours or until the lamb is very tender.

Garnish with the spring onions and serve immediately with steamed jasmine or Thai rice.

875 g (1¾ lb) **lamb leg** or **shoulder**, cut into large bite-sized pieces

500 ml (17 fl oz) **lamb stock**

3 tablespoons **massaman curry paste**

2 tablespoons **tamarind paste**

750 ml (1¼ pints) **coconut milk**

2 **lemon grass stalks**, bruised

16 **shallots**, peeled but left whole

350 g (11½ oz) **butternut squash**, peeled, deseeded and cut into bite-sized pieces

finely chopped **spring onions**, to garnish

Preparation time	**20 minutes**
Cooking temperature	**low**
Cooking time	**6¼–8¼ hours**
Serves	**4**
Heat rating	♪♪

Indonesian pork belly curry

2 tablespoons **sunflower oil**

800 g (1¾ lb) **belly pork**, cut into bite-sized pieces

10 **curry leaves**

1 tablespoon **cumin seeds**

1 tablespoon **crushed coriander seeds**

1 **onion**, finely chopped

2 teaspoons finely grated **garlic**

2 teaspoons peeled and finely grated **root ginger**

2 tablespoons **medium curry powder**

2 tablespoons **white wine vinegar**

2 **cinnamon sticks**

2 **star anise**

6 **green cardamom pods**, bruised

400 ml (14 fl oz) **coconut milk**

200 ml (7 fl oz) **water**

salt and **pepper**

Heat half the oil in a flameproof casserole over a medium-high heat and add the pork. Stir-fry for 4—5 minutes until browned. Remove with a slotted spoon and set aside.

Heat the remaining oil in the same casserole and add the curry leaves, cumin and coriander seeds, onion, garlic and ginger. Stir-fry for 3—4 minutes, then return the pork to the pan and add the curry powder. Stir-fry for 2—3 minutes until fragrant.

Transfer this mixture to the slow cooker pot. Stir in the vinegar, cinnamon, star anise, cardamom pods, coconut milk and measurement water. Season with salt and pepper and cover with the lid. Cook for 6—8 hours or until the pork is tender.

Serve hot with crusty bread.

Preparation time	**20 minutes**
Cooking temperature	**low**
Cooking time	**8½–10½ hours**
Serves	**4**
Heat rating	

Caribbean curried oxtail

1.5 kg (3 lb) **beef oxtail**, cut into large bite-sized pieces

2 tablespoons **vegetable oil**

2 teaspoons **ground mixed spice**

2 teaspoons **curry powder**

1.5 litres (2½ pints) **beef stock**

4 **carrots**, sliced

2 **onions**, finely chopped

3 **garlic cloves**, finely chopped

2 sprigs **thyme**

1 **Scotch bonnet chilli**, roughly chopped

400 g (13 oz) **tinned chopped tomatoes**

400 g (13 oz) **tinned butter beans**, rinsed and drained

salt and **pepper**

Bring a large saucepan of water to the boil. Add the oxtail and bring back to the boil. Reduce the heat slightly and simmer for 10–12 minutes. Remove from the pan with a slotted spoon and drain well on kitchen paper. Season with salt and pepper.

Heat the oil in heavy flameproof casserole and brown the oxtail on both sides for 6–8 minutes.

Transfer to the slow cooker pot. Add the mixed spice, curry powder, beef stock, carrots, onions, garlic, thyme, chilli, tomatoes and beans. Stir to mix well, cover with the lid and cook for 8–10 hours or until the oxtail is meltingly tender.

Serve immediately with rice.

Preparation time	**15 minutes**
Cooking temperature	**low**
Cooking time	**6½–8½ hours**
Serves	**4–6**
Heat rating	

Kashmiri almond, saffron & lamb curry

1 tablespoon **saffron threads**

300 ml (½ pint) **warm water**

4 tablespoons **vegetable oil**

3 **onions**, sliced

2 **garlic cloves**, finely diced

1 teaspoon finely grated **root ginger**

3 **dried Kashmiri red chillies**

8 **green cardamom pods**

1 teaspoon **fennel seeds**

½ teaspoon **ground turmeric**

2 teaspoons **ground cumin**

1 teaspoon **ground coriander**

1 teaspoon **garam masala**

1 kg (2 lb) boned **leg of lamb**, cut into bite-sized pieces

200 ml (7 fl oz) **double cream**

100 g (3½ oz) **toasted blanched almonds**

100 ml (3½ fl oz) **natural yogurt**, whisked

salt and **pepper**

Crumble the saffron into a small bowl, cover with the measurement water and leave to infuse.

Meanwhile, heat the oil in a large heavy saucepan over a medium heat. Add the onion, garlic, ginger and chillies, and fry for 8–10 minutes until the onions are soft. Add the cardamom pods, fennel seeds, turmeric, cumin, coriander and garam masala, and fry for 2–3 minutes until fragrant. Increase the heat, add the lamb and stir-fry for 6–8 minutes until the meat is well sealed and browned.

Transfer the lamb mixture to the slow cooker pot. Add the saffron and its soaking water, stir in the cream and season well with salt and pepper. Sprinkle in the almonds, cover with the lid and cook for 6–8 hours or until the lamb is meltingly tender.

Immediately before serving, stir in the yogurt and mix well.

Preparation time	**10 minutes**
Cooking temperature	**high**
Cooking time	**4¼–6¼ hours**
Serves	**4**
Heat rating	

4 tablespoons **sunflower oil**

750 g (1½ lb) **pork** or **chicken mince**

3 **garlic cloves**, minced

2 teaspoons peeled and finely grated **root ginger**

2 tablespoons **mild curry powder**

1 teaspoon **ground turmeric**

2 **green chillies**, chopped

400 ml (14 fl oz) **coconut milk**

2 **bay leaves**

200 g (7 oz) **fresh** or **frozen peas**

juice of 1 **lime**

salt and **pepper**

Filipino minced meat curry

Heat the oil in a large nonstick frying pan and brown the mince over a high heat for 3–4 minutes. Remove from the pan and set aside.

Add the garlic, ginger, curry powder, turmeric and green chillies to the pan, and stir-fry for 1–2 minutes until fragrant. Add the browned mince and stir to mix well.

Transfer the browned mince mixture to the slow cooker pot. Stir in the coconut milk, bay leaves and peas. Season with salt and pepper, cover with the lid and cook for 4–6 hours.

Just before serving, stir in the lime juice and serve over steamed rice or egg noodles.

Preparation time	**10 minutes**
Cooking temperature	**low**
Cooking time	**6¼–8¼ hours**
Serves	4
Heat rating	🌶

Burmese lamb curry

4 tablespoons **groundnut oil**

500 g (1 lb) boneless **lamb**, cubed

400 g (13 oz) **tinned chopped tomatoes**

2 teaspoons **ground turmeric**

2 tablespoons **mild curry paste**

300 g (10 oz) **baby new potatoes**

chopped **coriander leaves**, to garnish

Heat 1 tablespoon of the oil in a heavy saucepan over a medium-high heat and fry the lamb for 8–10 minutes until browned. Add the tomatoes, turmeric and curry paste, and stir to mix well.

Transfer this mixture to the slow cooker pot. Stir in the potatoes and the remaining oil, and pour over just enough water to cover the meat. Cover with the lid and cook for 6–8 hours or until the lamb is tender.

Garnish with the chopped coriander just before serving.

Preparation time	**5 minutes**
Cooking temperature	**low**
Cooking time	**6¼–8¼ hours**
Serves	**4**
Heat rating	

Rangoon beef & pumpkin curry

125 ml (4 fl oz) **vegetable oil**

4 tablespoons **mild curry paste**

750 g (1½ lb) **stewing beef**, cut into bite–sized chunks

500 g (1½ lb) **pumpkin**, peeled, deseeded and cut into 5 cm (2 inch) cubes

500 ml (17 fl oz) **water**

salt and **pepper**

Heat the oil in a deep frying pan or wok over a medium-high heat. Carefully add the curry paste (at this stage it will splutter), and stir it into the oil. Reduce the heat to low, and cook gently for about 10 minutes. If the mixture starts to burn, add a little water. When the paste is cooked, it should be a golden brown colour and have a little oil around the edges.

Add the beef and pumpkin to the pan and fry slowly, stirring, for 4–5 minutes.

Transfer this mixture to the slow cooker pot. Pour in the measurement water and stir through. Cover with the lid and cook for 6–8 hours or until the beef and pumpkin are tender.

Season well with salt and pepper, and serve hot with rice.

Preparation time	15 minutes
Cooking temperature	low
Cooking time	6¼–8¼ hours
Serves	4
Heat rating	🌶🌶🌶

Pork rendang

2 tablespoons **sunflower oil**

1 kg (2 lb) **pork tenderloin fillet**

2 **onions**, finely chopped

1 tablespoon **ground coriander**

1 teaspoon **ground turmeric**

6 **garlic cloves**, crushed

6 tablespoons very finely chopped **lemon grass** (remove tough outer leaves first)

2–3 **bird's-eye chillies**, chopped

4 tablespoons finely chopped **coriander** (including roots and stalks)

400 ml (14 fl oz) **coconut milk**

salt and **pepper**

Heat the oil in a deep heavy-based saucepan over a medium-high heat and brown the pork tenderloin fillet all over for 5–6 minutes.

Transfer to the slow cooker pot. Put the remaining ingredients in a food processor and blend until smooth. Season well with salt and pepper. Pour this mixture over the pork, cover with the lid and cook for 6–8 hours or until it is meltingly tender and most of the liquid has evaporated.

Remove the pork from the slow cooker pot and cut into slices. Serve with the juices spooned over steamed jasmine rice.

Preparation time	15 minutes
Cooking temperature	high
Cooking time	4–6 hours
Serves	4
Heat rating	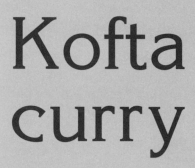

Kofta curry

750 g (1½ lb) **beef mince**

2 teaspoons peeled and finely grated **root ginger**

2 **garlic cloves**, minced

2 teaspoons **crushed fennel seeds**

1 teaspoon **ground cinnamon**

1 teaspoon **chilli powder**

500 ml (17 fl oz) **passata**

1 teaspoon **ground turmeric**

2 tablespoons **medium curry powder**

1 teaspoon **sugar**

salt and **pepper**

TO SERVE

100 ml (3½ fl oz) **natural yogurt**, whisked

pinch of **chilli powder**

chopped **mint leaves**

Put the mince in a bowl along with the ginger, garlic, fennel seeds, cinnamon and chilli powder. Season with salt and pepper. Using your hands, mix thoroughly until well combined. Form the mixture into small walnut-sized balls and set aside.

Pour the passata into the slow cooker pot and add the turmeric, curry powder and sugar. Carefully place the meatballs in the sauce, in a single layer. Cover with the lid and cook for 4–6 hours or until the sauce is thick and the meatballs are cooked through.

Serve immediately, drizzled with the yogurt, sprinkled with a pinch of chilli powder and garnished with mint leaves.

Preparation time	**15 minutes**
Cooking temperature	**high**
Cooking time	**4¼–6¼ hours**
Serves	**4**
Heat rating	

400 g (13 oz) **beef mince**

3 **garlic cloves**, minced

1 teaspoon peeled and finely grated **root ginger**

2 tablespoons **medium curry paste**

¼ teaspoon **ground turmeric**

4 tablespoons **vegetable oil or ghee**

1 large **onion**, peeled and finely chopped

10–12 **curry leaves**

2 **whole green chillies**, deseeded and chopped

6 ripe **tomatoes**, roughly chopped

200 ml (7 fl oz) **coconut milk**

4 tablespoons chopped **coriander leaves**

250 g (8 oz) **fresh** or **frozen peas**

salt

Kheema mutter

Put the beef mince in a bowl along with the garlic, ginger, curry paste and turmeric, and season with salt. Mix thoroughly using your fingers and set aside.

Heat the oil or ghee in a large frying pan over a medium heat. Add the onion, curry leaves and chillies, and stir-fry for 2–3 minutes. Increase the heat to high, add the beef mixture and stir-fry for 2–3 minutes.

Transfer this mixture to the slow cooker pot. Add the tomatoes, coconut milk, chopped coriander and peas, and stir to mix well. Cover with the lid and cook for 4–6 hours or until the pork is tender.

Serve immediately with warm naan bread.

Preparation time	**15 minutes**
Cooking temperature	**low**
Cooking time	**6¼–8¼ hours**
Serves	**4**
Heat rating	🌶🌶🌶

Caribbean lamb curry

Heat half the oil in a large heavy saucepan over a high heat. Brown the lamb in batches for 3–4 minutes until well sealed. Remove with a slotted spoon and set aside.

Heat the remaining oil in the same pan and add the onions, ginger, chilli, red pepper and spices. Stir-fry for 3–4 minutes until soft and fragrant.

Transfer to the slow cooker pot and add the lamb, tomatoes, lime zest and juice, and sugar. Season with salt and pepper. Cover with the lid and cook for 6–8 hours or until the lamb is tender.

Ladle into warm bowls and serve with rice.

2 tablespoons **sunflower oil**

625 g (1¼ lb) boned **leg of lamb**, cut into bite-sized cubes

2 **onions**, finely chopped

2 teaspoons peeled and finely grated **root ginger**

1 **Scotch bonnet chilli,** thinly sliced

1 **red pepper**, halved lengthways, deseeded and roughly chopped

2 teaspoons **ground mixed spice**

3 teaspoons **ground cumin**

1 **cinnamon stick**

pinch of grated **nutmeg**

400 g (13 oz) **tinned chopped tomatoes**

finely grated zest and juice of 2 **limes**

50 g (2 oz) **soft light brown sugar**

salt and **pepper**

Preparation time	10 minutes, plus marinating
Cooking temperature	low
Cooking time	6¼–8¼ hours
Serves	4
Heat rating	🌶 🌶 🌶

750 g (1½ lb) **goat** or **mutton**, cut into bite-sized cubes

1 teaspoon **salt**

2 tablespoons **thyme leaves**

1 teaspoon **pepper**

3 tablespoons **ground coriander**

2 tablespoons **turmeric**

½ teaspoon **ground fenugreek seeds**

2 tablespoons **ground ginger**

1 teaspoon **ground cardamom seeds**

2 teaspoons **ground cinnamon**

2 tablespoons **sunflower oil**

1 **onion**, sliced

750 ml (1¼ pints) **beef stock**

2 **Scotch bonnet chillies**, deseeded and chopped

3 large **potatoes**, peeled and cut into large chunks

Jamaican goat curry

Put the goat or mutton in a bowl. Mix together the salt, thyme, pepper and spices, and rub into the cubes of meat. Cover and marinate in the refrigerator for 6–8 hours or overnight if time permits.

Heat the oil in a heavy saucepan over a medium-low heat. Add the meat and onion, and cook, stirring, for 10–12 minutes until the meat is browned and well sealed.

Transfer the meat mixture to the slow cooker pot. Pour over the stock and add the chillies and potatoes. Cover with the lid and cook for 6–8 hours or until the meat is very tender.

Serve hot on a bed of rice.

Preparation time	15 minutes
Cooking temperature	low
Cooking time	6–8 hours
Serves	4
Heat rating	

Sindhi beef curry

Put the beef in a bowl, sprinkle over the cardamom, cloves, cinnamon and curry powder, and toss to mix well.

Transfer to the slow cooker pot along with the tomatoes, onions, garam masala and tomato purée. Pour over the measurement water and season well with salt and pepper. Cover with the lid and cook for 6–8 hours or until the meat is tender.

Serve the curry with a pilaf rice and pickles of your choice.

1 kg (2 lb) **stewing beef**, cut into bite-sized chunks

1 tablespoon **ground cardamom**

1/4 teaspoon **ground cloves**

1 teaspoon **ground cinnamon**

2 tablespoons **curry powder**

4 large **tomatoes**, roughly chopped

2 **red onions**, finely chopped

2 teaspoons **garam masala**

4 tablespoons **tomato purée**

750 ml (1 1/4 pints) **water**

salt and **pepper**

Preparation time	20 minutes
Cooking temperature	low
Cooking time	6¼–8¼ hours
Serves	4
Heat rating	🌶🌶

Cambodian pork & lemon grass curry

2 tablespoons **sunflower oil**

6 **shallots**, finely chopped

1 **red chilli**, thinly sliced

2 teaspoons peeled and finely grated **galangal**

2 tablespoons finely chopped **lemon grass** (remove tough outer leaves first)

2 teaspoons finely grated **garlic**

2 teaspoons **crushed fenugreek seeds**

1 tablespoon **ground cumin**

1 teaspoon **ground turmeric**

625 g (1¼ lb) **pork fillet**, cut into bite-sized pieces

1 tablespoon **tamarind paste**

finely grated zest and juice of 1 **lime**

400 ml (14 fl oz) **coconut milk**

8 **baby new potatoes**

2 **red peppers**, halved lengthways, deseeded and cut into bite-sized pieces

salt and **pepper**

Heat the oil in a large frying pan over a medium-high heat. Add the shallots, chilli, galangal, lemon grass, garlic, fenugreek seeds, cumin and turmeric, and stir-fry for 2–3 minutes until soft and fragrant. Add the pork and stir-fry for 3–4 minutes. Season well with salt and pepper.

Transfer this mixture to the slow cooker pot. Stir in the tamarind, lime zest and juice, coconut milk, potatoes and red peppers. Cover with the lid and cook for 6–8 hours or until the meat is tender.

Ladle into warm bowls and serve with rice.

Preparation time	**10 minutes, plus marinating**
Cooking temperature	**low**
Cooking time	**6¼–8¼ hours**
Serves	**4**
Heat rating	🌶🌶

875 g (1¾ lb) **mutton**, cut into bite-sized pieces

50 ml (2 fl oz) **white wine vinegar**

2 **onions**, roughly chopped

5 **garlic cloves**, chopped

2 tablespoons peeled and finely grated **root ginger**

75 ml (3 fl oz) **vegetable oil**

4 tablespoons **Sri Lankan curry powder**

10–12 **curry leaves**

500 ml (17 fl oz) **coconut milk**

Sri Lanka mutton curry

Put the mutton in a bowl. Pour over the vinegar and leave to marinate for 30 minutes.

In a food processor, blend the onions, garlic and ginger to a smooth paste. Heat the oil in a heavy saucepan over a medium heat and fry the paste for 2–3 minutes. Add the curry powder and curry leaves, and stir-fry for 3 minutes.

Drain the mutton from the marinade (reserving the marinade), and add the meat to the saucepan. Stir-fry for 5 minutes until well sealed.

Transfer the mutton mixture to the slow cooker pot and pour over the coconut milk and reserved marinade. Cover with the lid and cook for 6–8 hours or until the mutton is tender.

Preparation time	**10 minutes**
Cooking temperature	**low**
Cooking time	**6½–8½ hours**
Serves	**4**
Heat rating	

Spiced braised pork belly

Put the pork in a large heavy saucepan and cover with water. Place over a high heat and bring to the boil. Cover with a lid, reduce the heat and simmer gently for 30 minutes.

Drain the pork and transfer to the slow cooker pot with the remaining ingredients. Season with salt. Add just enough water to cover the pork belly pieces, cover with the lid and cook for 6–8 hours or until the pork is meltingly tender.

Serve the pork and its juices with steamed greens and steamed rice.

875 g (1¾ lb) **belly pork,** trimmed and cut into 12 pieces (ask your butcher to do this for you)

400 ml (14 fl oz) good-quality **beef stock**

75 ml (3 fl oz) **light soy sauce**

finely grated zest and juice of 1 large **orange**

1 tablespoon peeled and finely shredded **root ginger**

2 **garlic cloves**, sliced

1 tablespoon **hot chilli powder**

1 tablespoon **dark muscovado sugar**

3 **cinnamon sticks**

3 **whole cloves**

10 **whole black peppercorns**

2–3 **star anise**

salt

Preparation time	**20 minutes**
Cooking temperature	**low**
Cooking time	**6¼–8¼ hours**
Serves	**4**
Heat rating	

Moroccan spiced lamb shanks

2 tablespoons **light olive oil**

4 **lamb shanks**, trimmed of excess fat

2 teaspoons **ground cinnamon**

2 teaspoons **ground ginger**

2 teaspoons **ground cumin**

½ teaspoon **ground allspice**

¼ teaspoon freshly grated **nutmeg**

1 large **onion**, chopped

400 g (13 oz) **tinned chopped tomatoes**

1 teaspoon **salt**

about 250 ml (8 fl oz) **chicken stock** or **water**

Heat the oil in a flameproof casserole over a medium-high heat. Add the lamb shanks and fry for 6–8 minutes until well browned all over. Remove the shanks from the pan with a slotted spoon and set aside.

Reduce the heat slightly and add the spices to the casserole. Fry lightly in the oil for 1–2 minutes until fragrant. Add the onion and fry for a further 4–5 minutes.

Transfer the onion mixture to the slow cooker pot along with the lamb shanks (making sure that the lamb shanks stand snugly together in a single layer). Add the tomatoes, salt and enough stock or water to almost cover the shanks. Cover with the lid and cook for 6–8 hours or until the meat is almost falling off the bone.

Serve the lamb shanks and the sauce with couscous and harissa, if liked.

Preparation time	**15 minutes, plus marinating**
Cooking temperature	**low**
Cooking time	**6½–8½ hours**
Serves	**4**
Heat rating	

625 g (1¼ lb) **beef fillet**, cut into large bite-sized pieces

5 tablespoons **natural yogurt**

5 tablespoons **Madras curry powder**

2 tablespoons **sunflower oil**

1 large **onion**, halved and thinly sliced

3 **garlic cloves**, minced

1 teaspoon peeled and finely grated **root ginger**

200 g (7 oz) **tinned chopped tomatoes**

500 ml (17 fl oz) **coconut milk**

¼ teaspoon **garam masala**

salt

chopped **coriander leaves**, to garnish

Beef madras

Put the beef in a non-reactive bowl. Mix together the yogurt and curry powder, and pour over the beef. Season with salt, cover and leave to marinate in the refrigerator for 24 hours.

Heat the oil in a large nonstick wok or frying pan over a medium heat. Add the onion and stir-fry for 4–5 minutes until soft. Add the garlic and ginger, and stir-fry for a further 30 seconds. Reduce the heat to low and tip in the marinated beef. Stir-fry for 10–15 minutes.

Transfer this mixture to the slow cooker pot. Add the chopped tomatoes, coconut milk and garam masala. Cover with the lid and cook for 6–8 hours or until the beef is tender.

Garnish with the coriander leaves and serve with cooked basmati rice.

Preparation time	**10 minutes**
Cooking temperature	**low**
Cooking time	**6¼–8¼ hours**
Serves	4
Heat rating	🌶🌶

Burmese beef & potato curry

Heat the oils in a deep-sided frying pan over a medium-high heat. Carefully add the curry paste, reduce the heat to low and cook gently for about 3–4 minutes. If the mixture starts to burn, add a little water.

Stir in the cumin and coriander. Stir-fry for 30 seconds, then add the beef and stir-fry for 3–4 minutes. Season well with salt and pepper.

Transfer this mixture to the slow cooker pot. Add the potatoes and pour over the stock. Cover with the lid and cook for 6–8 hours or until the meat is tender and the potatoes are cooked through.

Serve immediately.

1 tablespoon **sesame oil**

100 ml (3½ fl oz) **vegetable oil**

3 tablespoons **medium curry paste**

1 teaspoon **ground cumin**

2 teaspoons **ground coriander**

750 g (1½ lb) **beef fillet**, cut into bite-sized pieces

400 g (13 oz) **potatoes**, peeled and cut into quarters

500 ml (17 fl oz) **chicken stock**

salt and **pepper**

Preparation time	**25 minutes, plus chilling**
Cooking temperature	**high**
Cooking time	**4–6 hours**
Serves	**4**
Heat rating	

Nonya pork curry

FOR THE MEATBALLS

1 small **egg**

2 teaspoons **cornflour**

2 **garlic cloves**, crushed

2 tablespoons finely chopped **coriander**

2 **red chillies**, finely chopped

875 g (1¾ lb) **pork mince**

salt and **pepper**

FOR THE NONYA CURRY PASTE

3 teaspoons finely grated **garlic**

100 g (3½ oz) **shallots**, finely chopped

1 teaspoon peeled and finely grated **galangal**

6 **long red chillies**, deseeded

4 tablespoons **sunflower oil**

400 g (13 oz) **tinned chopped tomatoes**

1 tablespoon **kecap asin** (or 1 tablespoon **dark soy sauce** and 1 teaspoon **fish sauce** such as nam pla)

400 ml (14 fl oz) **coconut milk**

Make the meatballs by combining all the ingredients together in a large bowl. Season well with salt and pepper, and roll tablespoons of the mixture into walnut-sized balls. Arrange side by side on a tray, cover and chill for 3—4 hours or overnight if time permits.

To make the curry paste, put the garlic, shallots, galangal, chillies and the oil in a blender or small food processor, and blend to a paste.

Transfer the paste mixture to the slow cooker pot. Add the tomatoes, kecap asin and coconut milk, and stir to mix well. (Kecap asin is a thick, salty Indonesian soy sauce and is available from many Asian or Oriental grocers — if it's hard to find, use the dark soy sauce and fish sauce mixture instead.)

Carefully add the meatballs to the curry sauce in a single layer, cover with the lid and cook for 4—6 hours.

Serve hot with steamed rice.

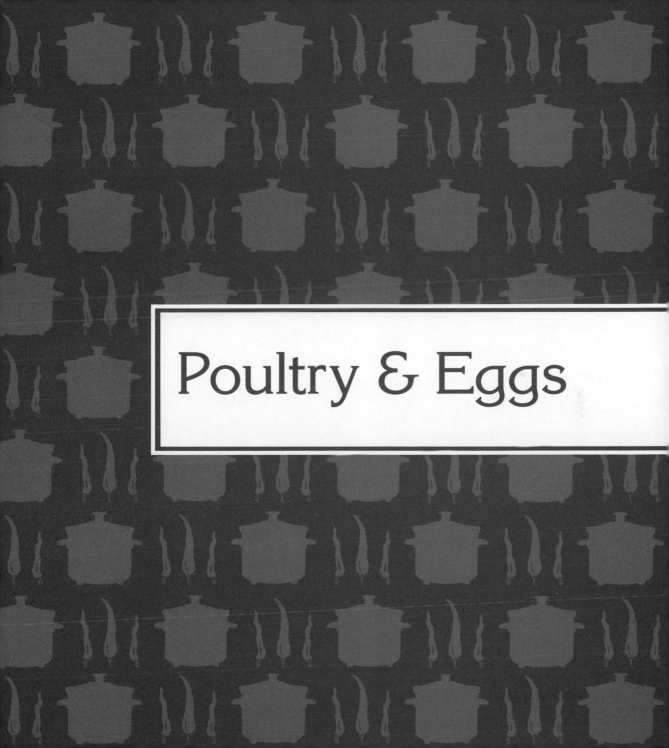

Poultry & Eggs

Preparation time	**15 minutes, plus standing**
Cooking temperature	**high**
Cooking time	**4–6 hours**
Serves	4
Heat rating	

2 **green mangoes**, peeled, stoned and cut into thin matchsticks

2 **red chillies**, roughly chopped

1 teaspoon **whole black peppercorns**

4 **candlenuts** or **macadamia nuts**

4 large skinless **chicken breast fillets**, sliced

250 ml (8 fl oz) **coconut milk**

400 ml (14 fl oz) **water**

1 teaspoon **palm sugar**

1 tablespoon **lime juice**

salt

3 tablespoons chopped **mint leaves**, to garnish

Balinese mango & chicken curry

Put the mangoes in a colander. Sprinkle the flesh with a little salt and leave to sweat for 20 minutes. Squeeze out the moisture and set aside.

Using a mortar and pestle, crush the chillies, peppercorns and candlenuts or macadamia nuts to a rough paste.

Put the chilli paste in the slow cooker pot along with the chicken, coconut milk, measurement water, palm sugar, reserved mango and lime juice. Season with salt and stir to mix well. Cover with the lid and cook for 4–6 hours or until cooked through and tender.

Serve hot garnished with the chopped mint leaves.

Preparation time	**10 minutes, plus marinating**
Cooking temperature	**low**
Cooking time	**6–8 hours**
Serves	**4–6**
Heat rating	🌶🌶🌶

Caribbean-style jerk chicken

Put all the ingredients for the jerk marinade in a food processor and blend to a smooth paste. Transfer to a glass or ceramic dish and toss the chicken pieces thoroughly in the marinade. Cover and leave to marinate overnight in the refrigerator.

Add the chicken pieces to the slow cooker pot with the stock, cover with the lid and cook for 6–8 hours or until very tender.

Serve immediately with rice and peas or bread.

1.5 kg (3 lb) **chicken thighs** and **drumsticks**

300 ml (½ pint) **chicken stock**

FOR THE CURRIED JERK MARINADE
1 tablespoon **curry powder**

2 **Scotch bonnet chillies**, roughly chopped

10 **spring onions**, roughly sliced

2 **onions**, roughly chopped

3 **garlic cloves**, roughly chopped

1 tablespoon peeled and finely grated **root ginger**

2 tablespoons **thyme leaves**

4 tablespoons **vegetable oil**

2 teaspoons **sugar**

2 teaspoons **salt**

200 ml (7 fl oz) **coconut cream**

Preparation time	**15 minutes**
Cooking temperature	**low**
Cooking time	**6-8 hours**
Serves	4
Heat rating	◢◢◢

2 **red chillies**, roughly chopped

2 **shallots**, roughly chopped

3 **garlic cloves**, chopped

2 tablespoons finely chopped **lemon grass** (remove tough outer leaves first)

1 tablespoon peeled and finely chopped **galangal** or **root ginger**

2 teaspoons **turmeric**

1 teaspoon **cayenne pepper**

1 teaspoon **ground coriander**

1 teaspoon **ground cumin**

¼ teaspoon **ground cinnamon**

3 tablespoons **fish sauce**

1 tablespoon **palm sugar**

4 **kaffir lime leaves**, finely shredded

400 ml (14 fl oz) **coconut milk**

juice of ½ **lime**

8 large **chicken drumsticks**

200 g (7 oz) **baby new potatoes**, peeled

10-12 **Thai sweet basil leaves**, to garnish

Thai yellow chicken curry

Put the chillies, shallots, garlic, lemon grass, galangal or ginger, turmeric, cayenne, ground coriander, cumin, cinnamon, fish sauce, palm sugar, kaffir lime leaves, coconut milk and lime juice in a food processor, and blend until fairly smooth.

Arrange the chicken drumsticks in a single layer in the slow cooker pot. Scatter over the potatoes. Pour over the yellow curry spice paste to coat the chicken and potatoes evenly. Cover with the lid and cook for 6–8 hours or until the chicken is cooked through.

Serve hot garnished with the basil leaves.

Preparation time	10 minutes
Cooking temperature	low
Cooking time	6¼–8¼ hours
Serves	4
Heat rating	🌶🌶

Bombay chicken curry

2 tablespoons **sunflower oil**

2 **onions**, chopped

2 **garlic cloves**, minced

1 teaspoon **ground ginger**

1 teaspoon **ground turmeric**

3 tablespoons **medium curry powder**

875 g (1¾ lb) **chicken thighs** (skin on)

400 g (13 oz) **tinned chopped tomatoes**

400 ml (14 fl oz) **coconut milk**

salt

Heat half the oil in a large saucepan over a medium heat. Add the onions and fry for 6–8 minutes until soft and golden. Add the garlic and spices, and cook for 1 minute, stirring often, until fragrant. Tip out onto a plate and set aside.

Heat the remaining oil in the same pan over a medium-high heat, and brown the chicken on all sides for 5–6 minutes until nicely coloured. Add the reserved onion mixture and cook, stirring with a wooden spoon, for 1 minute until the chicken is coated in the mixture.

Transfer this mixture to the slow cooker pot. Add the tomatoes and coconut milk, season with salt and stir to mix well. Cover with the lid and cook for 6–8 hours or until the chicken is tender.

Preparation time	**20 minutes**
Cooking temperature	**low**
Cooking time	**6¼–8¼ hours**
Serves	**4**
Heat rating	

Duck jungle curry

2 tablespoons **sunflower oil**

625 g (1¼ lb) **duck breasts**, sliced into thin strips

400 ml (14 fl oz) **chicken stock**

1 tablespoon **fish sauce** such as nam pla

65 g (2½ oz) **tinned bamboo shoots**, rinsed and drained

200 g (7 oz) **pea aubergines**

small handful of **Thai holy basil leaves**, plus extra to garnish

FOR THE JUNGLE CURRY PASTE

1 tablespoon **ground white peppercorns**

4 **green chillies**, finely chopped

2 teaspoons peeled and finely grated **galangal**

2 tablespoons very finely chopped **lemon grass** (remove tough outer leaves first)

3 **kaffir lime leaves**, very finely shredded

1 teaspoon **shrimp paste**

6 **garlic cloves**, crushed

5 **Thai shallots**, finely chopped

3 tablespoons finely chopped **coriander root**

4 tablespoons **sunflower oil**

To make the curry paste, put all the paste ingredients in a small food processor and blend to a smooth paste (add a little water if needed). (Good-quality, ready-made curry pastes are available in many supermarkets and Asian and Oriental grocers — a ready-made jungle curry paste can be used in this recipe to save time.)

Heat the oil in a large nonstick wok over a high heat. Add the curry paste and stir-fry for 1–2 minutes. Add the duck and stir-fry for 4–5 minutes until sealed.

Transfer this mixture to the slow cooker pot. Pour over the stock and fish sauce, and add the bamboo shoots, pea aubergines and basil leaves. Cover with the lid and cook for 6–8 hours.

Ladle the curry into bowls, garnish with the remaining basil leaves and serve immediately with steamed jasmine rice.

Preparation time	10 minutes, plus marinating
Cooking temperature	low
Cooking time	6¼–8¼ hours
Serves	4
Heat rating	🌶 🌶 🌶

875 g (1¾ lb) **chicken drumsticks** and **thighs**

3 tablespoons **hot curry powder**

3 tablespoons **vegetable oil**

4 **garlic cloves**, minced

1 **onion**, sliced

4 small **tomatoes**, chopped

2 **chicken stock cubes**

750 ml (1¼ pints) **coconut milk**

3 **potatoes**, peeled and quartered

chopped **coriander leaves**, to garnish

Hong Kong-style chicken curry

Put the chicken in a non-reactive bowl and sprinkle over the curry powder. Toss to mix well and leave to marinate in the refrigerator for 30 minutes.

Heat the oil in a large saucepan over a medium heat. Add the garlic, onion and tomatoes, and fry for 3–4 minutes. Crumble in the stock cubes and add the marinated chicken. Stir-fry for 4–5 minutes.

Transfer the chicken mixture to the slow cooker pot. Pour over the coconut milk and add the potatoes. Cover with the lid and cook for 6–8 hours or until the chicken is tender.

Garnish with the coriander leaves and serve hot with rice and chutney or pickle, if liked.

Preparation time	10 minutes
Cooking temperature	low
Cooking time	6¼–8¼ hours
Serves	4
Heat rating	🌶🌶

Burmese-style
tomato & chicken curry

Heat the oil in a medium frying pan over a low heat and stir-fry the shallots for 6–8 minutes until soft and lightly golden. Remove from the pan with a slotted spoon (reserving the oil in the pan) and set aside.

Put the chicken in the frying pan with the reserved oil and stir in the curry paste and curry powder until evenly coated.

Transfer to the slow cooker pot. Pour in enough water to just cover the chicken and add the coconut milk, tomato purée, fish sauce, palm sugar and tomato wedges. Cover with the lid and cook for 6–8 hours.

Garnish with the coriander leaves and serve immediately with jasmine rice.

100 ml (3½ fl oz) **vegetable oil**

8 **shallots**, thinly sliced

500 g (1 lb) **skinless chicken thigh fillets**, cut into large pieces

1 tablespoon **Thai red curry paste**

1 tablespoon **mild curry powder**

125 ml (4 fl oz) **coconut milk**

4 tablespoons **tomato purée**

2 tablespoons **fish sauce** such as nam pla

1 tablespoon **palm sugar**

3 large, ripe **tomatoes**, cut into wedges

roughly chopped **coriander leaves**, to garnish

Preparation time	25 minutes, plus marinating
Cooking temperature	low
Cooking time	6½–8½ hours
Serves	4
Heat rating	

Butter chicken

150 g (5 oz) unsalted raw cashew nuts

1 tablespoon **fennel seeds**

4 tablespoons **curry powder**

4 **garlic cloves**, crushed

2 teaspoons peeled and finely grated **root ginger**

2 tablespoons **white wine vinegar**

100 ml (3½ fl oz) **tomato purée**

150 ml (¼ pint) **natural yogurt**

1 kg (2 lb) **skinless chicken thigh fillets**, cut into large bite-sized pieces

50 g (2 oz) **butter**

1 large **onion**, finely chopped

1 **cassia bark** or **cinnamon stick**

4 **green cardamom pods**

1 teaspoon **chilli powder**

400 g (13 oz) **tinned chopped tomatoes**

150 ml (¼ pint) **chicken stock**

100 ml (3½ fl oz) **single cream**

salt and **pepper**

In a nonstick frying pan, dry-roast the cashew nuts, fennel seeds and curry powder for 1–2 minutes until very aromatic. Transfer to a clean coffee grinder and grind to a fine powder.

Put the ground spices in a blender or food processor with the garlic, ginger, vinegar, tomato purée and half the yogurt, and blend until smooth. Transfer to a large non-reactive bowl along with the remaining yogurt and the chicken. Toss to mix well, then cover and leave to marinate in the refrigerator for 24 hours.

To cook, melt the butter in a large nonstick wok or saucepan over a medium heat. Add the onion, cassia bark or cinnamon, and cardamom pods. Stir-fry for 6–8 minutes until the onion is soft and translucent. Add the chicken mixture and cook, stirring, for 10 minutes. Season well with salt and pepper.

Transfer this mixture to the slow cooker pot. Stir in the chilli powder, chopped tomatoes, stock and cream. Cover with the lid and cook for 6–8 hours or until tender.

Serve immediately with rice or warm naan bread.

Preparation time	**15 minutes**
Cooking temperature	**low**
Cooking time	**6¼–8¼ hours**
Serves	4
Heat rating	

2–3 tablespoons **vegetable oil**

3 **garlic cloves**, crushed

1 large **onion**, quartered

1 tablespoon **fish sauce**

3 tablespoons **curry powder**

400 ml (14 fl oz) **water**

4 large **potatoes**, peeled and cut into large, bite-sized pieces

1 **red pepper**, halved lengthways, deseeded and cut into big squares

3 **celery sticks**, cut into 3 cm (1¼ inch) lengths

400 ml (14 fl oz) **coconut milk**

4 **hard-boiled eggs**, peeled

salt and **pepper**

Filipino egg & potato curry

Heat the oil in a large frying pan over a medium-high heat. Add the garlic and onion and fry for a few minutes until soft.

Transfer this mixture to the slow cooker pot. Pour in the fish sauce and sprinkle over the curry powder. Add the measurement water, potatoes, red pepper, celery, coconut milk and eggs. Season well. Cover with the lid and cook for 6–8 hours or until the sauce has thickened.

Serve with rice or bread.

Preparation time	**15 minutes**
Cooking temperature	**low**
Cooking time	**6¼–8¼ hours**
Serves	**4**
Heat rating	

Singapore chicken curry

Put the onions, garlic and ginger in a small food processor. Add the measurement water and blend to a paste.

Heat the oil in a frying pan or wok over a medium heat. Add the onion paste and stir-fry for 3–4 minutes. Sprinkle over the curry powder and stir-fry for a further 3–4 minutes until fragrant.

Place the chicken in the slow cooker pot. Stir in the coconut milk, lemon grass, kaffir lime leaves, tamarind paste and potatoes. Season well with salt and pepper. Cover with the lid and cook for 6–8 hours or until the chicken and potatoes are tender.

Immediately before serving, stir in the coriander and serve with steamed rice.

2 **onions,** finely chopped

6 **garlic cloves,** roughly chopped

1 tablespoon peeled and finely grated **root ginger**

6–8 tablespoons **water**

75 ml (3 fl oz) **vegetable oil**

6 tablespoons **medium curry powder**

875 g (1¾ lb) **skinless chicken thigh fillets,** cut into bite-sized pieces

400 ml (14 fl oz) **coconut milk**

2 **lemon grass stalks,** bruised

8–10 **kaffir lime leaves**

1 tablespoon **tamarind paste**

400 g (13 oz) **potatoes,** peeled and cut into bite-sized pieces

small handful of chopped **coriander leaves**

salt and **pepper**

Preparation time	**10 minutes**
Cooking temperature	**low**
Cooking time	**6–8 hours**
Serves	**4**
Heat rating	

Penang red curry

875 g (1¾ lb) **chicken thighs** and **drumsticks**

3 **tomatoes**, cut into wedges

2 **red peppers**, halved lengthways, deseeded and thinly sliced

Thai sweet basil leaves, to garnish

FOR THE PENANG RED CURRY PASTE

4 tablespoons **tomato paste**

1 small **onion**, peeled and quartered

1 tablespoon finely grated **root ginger**

3 cloves **garlic**

2 tablespoons **soy sauce**

2 tablespoons **fish sauce**

1 teaspoon **shrimp paste**

1 tablespoon **paprika**

2 tablespoons **chilli powder**

2 tablespoons **ground coriander**

1–2 **red chillies**

½ teaspoon **turmeric**

1 tablespoon **ground cumin**

2 **kaffir lime leaves**

½ teaspoon **cinnamon**

¼ teaspoon **ground nutmeg**

¼ teaspoon **ground cloves**

400 ml (14 fl oz) **coconut milk**

juice of ½ **lime**

Place all the ingredients for the Penang red curry paste in a food processor and blend until smooth.

Arrange the chicken pieces in a single layer in the slow cooker pot and add the tomatoes and peppers. Pour over the Penang red curry paste, cover with the lid and cook for 6—8 hours or until the chicken is tender.

Garnished with a few basil leaves and serve hot with steamed jasmine rice.

Preparation time	**15 minutes**
Cooking temperature	**high**
Cooking time	**4¼–6¼ hours**
Serves	**4**
Heat rating	✎ ✎ ✎

3 tablespoons **vegetable oil**

500 g (1 lb) **minced chicken**

2 **onions**, thinly sliced

2 **red chillies**, deseeded and thinly sliced

6–8 **curry leaves**

3 **garlic cloves**, minced

1 teaspoon peeled and finely grated **root ginger**

1 tablespoon **ground coriander**

2 tablespoons **medium** or **hot curry powder**

4 **tomatoes**, roughly chopped

200 g (7 oz) **fresh** or **frozen peas**

juice of 1 **lemon**

small handful of chopped **mint leaves**

small handful of chopped **coriander**

salt

Chicken balti

Heat the oil in a large wok or frying pan over a medium heat. Add the minced chicken, onions, chillies and curry leaves, and stir-fry for 4–5 minutes or until the chicken has browned.

Transfer to the slow cooker pot. Add the garlic, ginger, coriander, curry powder, tomatoes and peas, and stir to mix well. Cover with the lid and cook for 4–6 hours or until the mixture is tender.

Just before serving, stir in the lemon juice and chopped herbs. Season with salt and serve immediately with naan bread or rice.

Preparation time	**10 minutes, plus marinating**
Cooking temperature	**low**
Cooking time	**6¼–8¼ hours**
Serves	**4**
Heat rating	

Malaysian chicken curry

20 **Thai shallots**, peeled and roughly chopped

1.5 cm (¾ inch) piece of **root ginger**, peeled and roughly chopped

2 **garlic cloves**, minced

875 g (1¾ lb) **chicken thighs**

3 tablespoons **vegetable oil**

2 **cinnamon sticks**

2 **whole cloves**

2 **star anise**

2 tablespoons **medium curry paste**

300 ml (½ pint) **coconut milk**

2 large **potatoes**, peeled and roughly chopped

Blend half the shallots with the ginger and garlic in a food processor until fairly smooth. Put the chicken in a wide bowl. Spread the shallot paste all over the chicken and set aside to marinate for 15–20 minutes.

Heat the oil in a large wok or frying pan over a medium-high heat and fry the remaining shallots, cinnamon, cloves and star anise for 2–3 minutes until fragrant. Add the curry paste and stir-fry for 2–3 minutes, then add the paste-covered chicken and stir-fry for a further 4–5 minutes.

Transfer the chicken mixture to the slow cooker pot. Pour over the coconut milk and just enough water to cover the chicken. Add the potatoes, cover with the lid and cook for 6–8 hours or until fragrant and tender.

Preparation time	10 minutes
Cooking temperature	low
Cooking time	6¼–8¼ hours
Serves	4
Heat rating	🌶🌶🌶

Thai green chicken curry

1 tablespoon **sunflower oil**

3 tablespoons **Thai green curry paste**

2 **green chillies**, finely chopped

875 g (1¾ lb) **skinless chicken thigh fillets**, cut into bite-sized pieces

400 ml (14 fl oz) **coconut milk**

200 ml (7 fl oz) **chicken stock**

6 **kaffir lime leaves**

2 tablespoons **fish sauce** such as nam pla

1 tablespoon grated **palm sugar**

200 g (7 oz) **pea aubergines** (or 1 large **aubergine**, cut into bite-sized cubes)

100 g (3½ oz) **green beans**, trimmed

50 g (2 oz) **tinned bamboo shoots**, rinsed and drained

large handful of **Thai sweet basil leaves**

large handful of **coriander leaves**

juice of 1 **lime**

Heat the oil in a large nonstick wok or saucepan over a medium-high heat. Add the green curry paste and green chillies and stir-fry for 2–3 minutes. Add the chicken and stir-fry for 5–6 minutes until the chicken is sealed and lightly browned.

Transfer the chicken mixture to the slow cooker pot. Stir in the coconut milk, stock, kaffir lime leaves, fish sauce, palm sugar, pea aubergines, green beans and bamboo shoots. (If pea aubergines are hard to find, use a large aubergine cut into bite-sized cubes instead.) Cover with the lid and cook for 6–8 hours or until tender.

Stir in the herbs and lime juice. Serve in warm bowls with steamed jasmine rice.

Preparation time	**20 minutes, plus marinating**
Cooking temperature	**high**
Cooking time	**4–6 hours**
Serves	**4**
Heat rating	🌶🌶

1 medium **chicken**, about 875 g (1¾ lb), jointed and skin on

4 teaspoons peeled and finely grated **root ginger**

6 **garlic cloves**, minced

2 teaspoons **ground turmeric**

1 tablespoon **paprika**

2 teaspoons **ground cinnamon**

juice of 2 **limes**

4 tablespoons **sunflower oil**

2 teaspoons **ground cumin**

1 tablespoon **ground coriander**

2 teaspoons **dried chilli flakes**

100 ml (3½ fl oz) **natural yogurt**, whisked

1 tablespoon **runny honey**

200 ml (7 fl oz) **water**

salt and **pepper**

African-style 'roast' curried chicken

Put the chicken in a large mixing bowl. Mix together the remaining ingredients, season well with salt and pepper, and pour over the chicken. Mix well to combine, cover and leave to marinate in the refrigerator for 6–8 hours or overnight if possible.

Place the chicken mixture in the slow cooker pot with the measurement water. Cover with the lid and cook for 4–6 hours or until the chicken is tender.

Serve the chicken with a crisp green salad and bread.

Preparation time	**10 minutes**
Cooking temperature	**low**
Cooking time	**6¼–8¼ hours**
Serves	4
Heat rating	🌶🌶

Chicken massaman

Heat the oil in a frying pan over a medium heat. Add the onion and chicken and stir-fry for 6–8 minutes.

Transfer to the slow cooker pot. Blend the curry paste with a little of the coconut milk and add to the pot with the remaining coconut milk, fish sauce, lime juice, sugar and aubergines. Stir to mix well. Cover with the lid and cook for 6–8 hours or until the chicken is tender.

Stir through the chopped basil and serve immediately with steamed Thai or jasmine rice.

2 tablespoons **vegetable oil**

1 large **onion**, sliced

875 g (1¾ lb) skinless **chicken breast fillets**, cut into bite-sized cubes

6 tablespoons **massaman curry paste**

500 ml (17 fl oz) **coconut milk**

2 tablespoons **fish sauce** such as nam pla

2 tablespoons **lime juice**

1 teaspoon **sugar**

100 g (3½ oz) **Thai aubergines**

2 tablespoons chopped **Thai sweet basil**

Preparation time	**10 minutes**
Cooking temperature	**low**
Cooking time	**6¼–8¼ hours**
Serves	**4**
Heat rating	

South Indian egg curry

2 tablespoons **sunflower oil**

1 tablespoon **cumin seeds**

1 tablespoon **black mustard seeds**

2 **garlic cloves**, minced

2 **dried red chillies**

10 **curry leaves**

1 **onion**, halved and thinly sliced

1 teaspoon **chilli powder**

1 tablespoon **ground coriander**

½ teaspoon **ground turmeric**

200 g (7 oz) **tinned chopped tomatoes**

1 teaspoon **sugar**

400 ml (14 fl oz) **coconut milk**

6 **hard-boiled eggs**, peeled

2 peeled and boiled **potatoes**, cut into small bite-sized pieces

salt

chopped **coriander leaves**, to garnish

Heat the oil in a large nonstick wok or frying pan over a medium-high heat. Add the cumin and mustard seeds and stir-fry for 30–40 seconds until the mustard seeds have started to pop.

Add the garlic, chillies and curry leaves and fry for 1 minute. Reduce the heat to medium, add the onion and fry, stirring constantly, for 5–6 minutes until soft.

Transfer this mixture to the slow cooker pot. Stir in the chilli powder, ground coriander and turmeric, then stir in the tomatoes, sugar, coconut milk, eggs and potatoes. Season with salt. Cover with the lid and cook for 6–8 hours until the sauce has thickened.

Garnish with coriander leaves and serve immediately with crusty bread or steamed rice.

Preparation time	5 minutes
Cooking temperature	high
Cooking time	4¼–6¼ hours
Serves	4
Heat rating	🌶

2 tablespoons **sunflower oil**

1 **onion**, chopped

2 **garlic cloves**, crushed

250 g (8 oz) **potatoes**, peeled and cut into 1.5 cm (¾ inch) cubes

500 g (1 lb) **minced chicken**

200 g (7 oz) **frozen peas**

1 tablespoon **korma curry paste** or **powder**

200 ml (7 fl oz) **vegetable stock**

2 tablespoons **mango chutney**

salt and **pepper**

chopped **coriander leaves**, to garnish

Chicken korma

Heat the oil in a saucepan over a medium heat. Add the onion and garlic and fry for 5 minutes until soft and starting to colour. Add the potatoes and chicken and stir-fry for a further 5 minutes until the meat has browned.

Transfer this mixture into the slow cooker pot, add the rest of the ingredients and season with salt and pepper. Cover with the lid and cook for 4–6 hours.

Garnish with coriander leaves and serve with yogurt and steamed rice.

Preparation time	**10 minutes**
Cooking temperature	**low**
Cooking time	**6¼–8¼ hours**
Serves	4
Heat rating	🌶🌶🌶

Green duck curry
with carrots & pea aubergines

Heat the oil in a large nonstick wok or saucepan over a medium-high heat. Add the green curry paste and chillies, and stir-fry for 2–3 minutes. Add the duck and stir-fry for 5–6 minutes until the meat is well sealed and lightly browned.

Transfer to the slow cooker pot. Stir in the coconut milk, stock, kaffir lime leaves, fish sauce, palm sugar, pea aubergines and carrots. Cover with the lid and cook for 6–8 hours or until tender.

Stir in the herbs and lime juice. Serve the curry in warm bowls with steamed jasmine rice.

1 tablespoon **sunflower oil**

3 tablespoons **Thai green curry paste**

2 **green chillies**, finely chopped

875 g (1¾ lb) **duck breast fillets**, skinned and cut into bite-sized pieces

400 ml (14 fl oz) **coconut milk**

200 ml (7 fl oz) **chicken stock**

6 **kaffir lime leaves**

2 tablespoons **fish sauce** such as nam pla

1 tablespoon grated **palm sugar**

200 g (7 oz) **pea aubergines**

200 g (7 oz) **carrots**, peeled and cut into bite-sized pieces

large handful of **Thai sweet basil leaves**

large handful of **coriander leaves**

juice of 1 **lime**

Preparation time	**20 minutes, plus marinating**
Cooking temperature	**low**
Cooking time	**6¼–8¼ hours**
Serves	**4**
Heat rating	🌶🌶🌶

Goan chicken xacutti

1 kg (2 lb) **chicken thighs** and **drumsticks**

2 tablespoons **desiccated coconut**

1 tablespoon **vegetable oil**

2 large **onions**, finely chopped

1 tablespoon **tomato purée**

4 **red chillies**, left whole

1 teaspoon **ground cloves**

2 tablespoons **garam masala**

1 **cinnamon stick**

500 ml (17 fl oz) **water**

chopped **coriander leaves**, to garnish

lime wedges, to serve

FOR THE XACUTTI MARINADE

1 tablespoon **garlic purée**

1 tablespoon **ginger purée**

2 tablespoons **coriander**, finely chopped

1 tablespoon **tamarind paste**

1 teaspoon **ground turmeric**

1 teaspoon **chilli powder**

To make the xacutti marinade, mix together all the marinade ingredients in a large bowl. Add the chicken and toss to coat well. Cover and leave to marinate in the refrigerator for 6–8 hours, or overnight if time permits.

Heat a small frying pan without oil over a low heat and dry-roast the coconut for a few minutes until lightly golden. Remove from the heat and set aside.

Heat the oil in a heavy saucepan over a medium heat and fry the onions for 8–10 minutes until soft and lightly browned. Add the roasted coconut, tomato purée, chillies, ground cloves, garam masala and cinnamon stick. Stir well to blend. Add the chicken pieces with the marinade and continue to stir-fry over a high heat for 5 minutes.

Transfer this mixture to the slow cooker pot. Pour over the measurement water and stir to mix well. Cover with the lid and cook for 6–8 hours or until the chicken is tender.

Garnish with some chopped coriander and serve hot with lime wedges for squeezing over.

Preparation time	15 minutes
Cooking temperature	low
Cooking time	6¼–8¼ hours
Serves	4
Heat rating	🌶 🌶

2 tablespoons **sunflower oil**

1 **onion**, halved and thinly sliced

2 teaspoons **brown mustard seeds**

2 teaspoons finely grated **garlic**

1 teaspoon **ground turmeric**

2 teaspoons **ground coriander**

2 tablespoons **curry powder**

750g (1½ lb) **skinless chicken thigh fillets**

250 ml (8 fl oz) **water**

12–16 **cherry tomatoes**

salt and **pepper**

Bangladeshi chicken curry

Heat the oil in a large nonstick wok or frying pan over a medium heat. Add the onion and stir-fry for 5–6 minutes until soft.

Meanwhile, using a mortar and pestle, pound the mustard seeds and garlic into a rough paste, and add to the pan. Stir-fry for 1 minute, then add the turmeric, ground coriander and curry powder. Stir-fry for 2–3 minutes until fragrant. Add the chicken and stir-fry over a high heat for 5 minutes.

Transfer to the slow cooker pot. Pour over the measurement water and add the cherry tomatoes. Season well with salt and pepper. Cover with the lid and cook for 6–8 hours or until tender.

Preparation time	**10 minutes**
Cooking temperature	**low**
Cooking time	**6¼–8¼ hours**
Serves	**4**
Heat rating	

Fruity Lebanese egg & chicken curry

Heat the oil in a deep saucepan over a medium heat. Add the onion and fry for about 5 minutes until soft. Add the garlic and curry powder and stir-fry for 1–2 minutes until fragrant. Add the chicken and fry for 5 minutes until lightly golden.

Transfer this mixture to the slow cooker pot. Add the apples, tomato purée, coconut milk and stock.

Mix the cornflour with the measurement water and add to the pot with the eggs. Cover with the lid and cook for 6–8 hours or until tender.

Serve immediately with rice.

3 tablespoons **vegetable oil**

1 **onion**, chopped

2 **garlic cloves**, minced

2 tablespoons **curry powder**

350 g (11½ oz) **skinless chicken breast fillets**, cut into bite-sized cubes

2 **apples**, peeled, cored and roughly diced

1 tablespoon **tomato purée**

250 ml (8 fl oz) **coconut milk**

750 ml (1¼ pints) **chicken stock**

2 tablespoons **cornflour**

2 tablespoons **cold water**

4 **hard-boiled eggs**, peeled

Preparation time	**15 minutes**
Cooking temperature	**low**
Cooking time	**6–8 hours**
Serves	**4**
Heat rating	

Indonesian chicken curry

2 **red chillies**

5 **candlenuts** or **macadamia nuts**

½ large **onion**, roughly chopped

3 **garlic cloves**, chopped

1 tablespoon **ground coriander**

1 teaspoon **fennel seeds**

2 teaspoons peeled and finely chopped **galangal**

1 teaspoon **shrimp paste**

875 g (1¾ lb) **chicken thigh fillets**

500 ml (17 fl oz) **coconut milk**

1 tablespoon **tamarind paste**

2 tablespoons finely chopped **lemon grass** (remove tough outer leaves first)

2 **kaffir lime leaves**

1 teaspoon **salt**

1 teaspoon **palm sugar**

2 tablespoons **desiccated coconut**

Put the chillies, candlenuts or macadamia nuts, onion, garlic, coriander, fennel seeds, galangal and shrimp paste in a blender or small food processor and blend until fairly smooth (adding a little water if needed).

Put the chicken in the slow cooker pot. Pour over the coconut milk, add the tamarind paste, lemon grass, kaffir lime leaves, salt and palm sugar. Cover with the lid and cook for 6—8 hours or until tender.

Just before serving, roast the desiccated coconut for 2—3 minutes until lightly golden in a small, dry frying pan over a medium-low heat. Watch carefully to make sure that it doesn't scorch. Sprinkle the desiccated coconut over the chicken curry and serve hot with rice.

Preparation time	**20 minutes**
Cooking temperature	**high**
Cooking time	**4½–6½ hours**
Serves	**4**
Heat rating	

875 g (1¾ lb) **minced chicken**

100 g (3½ oz) **fresh breadcrumbs**

75 g (3 oz) **coriander**, chopped

4 tablespoons finely chopped **lemon grass** (remove tough outer leaves first)

3 **red chillies**, deseeded and finely chopped

2 tablespoons **vegetable oil**

2–3 tablespoons **Thai red curry paste**

400 ml (14 fl oz) **coconut milk**

1 tablespoon **tomato purée**

salt and **pepper**

Thai chicken meatball curry

Mix together the minced chicken, breadcrumbs, half the chopped coriander, lemon grass and chillies. Season with salt and pepper. Divide the mixture into walnut-sized balls.

Heat the oil in a wok over a medium heat. Gently fry the meatballs gently for about 10 minutes, turning once, until lightly browned (this can be done in two batches using 1 tablespoon oil for each batch).

Transfer the meatballs to the slow cooker pot in a single layer. Mix together the red curry paste, coconut milk and tomato purée and pour over the meatballs in the pot. Season with salt, cover with the lid and cook for 4–6 hours or until the meatballs are cooked through.

Scatter with the remaining coriander and serve immediately.

Preparation time	**10 minutes**
Cooking temperature	**high**
Cooking time	**4¼–6¼ hours**
Serves	4
Heat rating	🌶🌶🌶

Sri Lankan egg curry

Heat the oil in a frying pan over a medium heat. Prick the eggs all over with a fork and fry for a few minutes until evenly browned. Remove with a slotted spoon, drain on kitchen paper and set aside.

Reheat the oil and add the onion, curry leaves, garlic, ginger and chillies. Stir-fry over a medium heat for 6–8 minutes. Sprinkle over the curry powder and stir-fry for 1–2 minutes until fragrant. Stir in the chopped tomatoes, season with salt and stir to mix well.

Transfer the eggs to the slow cooker pot and pour over the spiced tomato mixture. Cover with the lid and cook for 4–6 hours.

Stir in the coriander and serve immediately.

4 tablespoons **vegetable oil**

6 **hard-boiled eggs**, peeled

1 **onion**, finely chopped

10 **curry leaves**

3 **garlic cloves**, finely chopped

2 teaspoons peeled and finely grated **root ginger**

2 **green chillies**, finely chopped

3 tablespoons **medium curry powder**

300 g (10 oz) **tinned chopped tomatoes**

6 tablespoons finely chopped **coriander leaves**

salt

Preparation time	**10 minutes**
Cooking temperature	**low**
Cooking time	**6½–8½ hours**
Serves	**4**
Heat rating	🌶🌶🌶

Chettinad chicken

4 tablespoons **ghee** or **vegetable oil**

2 **bay leaves**

8 **green cardamom pods**

1 **cinnamon stick**

1 teaspoon **fennel seeds**

2 teaspoons **cumin seeds**

20 **whole black peppercorns**

6–8 **dried red chillies**

3 **whole cloves**

15–20 **curry leaves**

2 **onions**, finely chopped

4 tablespoons **Madras curry powder** or **paste**

1 **tomato**, chopped

875 g (1¾ lb) **chicken thighs** (bone in)

natural yogurt, lightly whisked, to serve

Heat the ghee or oil in a large saucepan over a medium-high heat. When hot, add the bay leaves, cardamom pods, cinnamon, fennel and cumin seeds, peppercorns, chillies and cloves. Stir-fry for 1–2 minutes until fragrant.

Add the curry leaves and onions, and stir-fry for 8–10 minutes until the onions are soft and just lightly coloured. Add the Madras curry powder or paste and continue stir-frying for 4–6 minutes, adding a little water to prevent sticking. Add the tomato, including any juices, and stir-fry for a further 3–4 minutes until the tomato has broken down.

Place the chicken thighs in the slow cooker pot and spoon over the onion and spice mixture. Stir until they are well coated, then add just enough water to cover. Cover with the lid and cook for 6–8 hours or until the chicken is tender.

Serve hot with rice and the yogurt.

Preparation time	**20 minutes, plus chilling**
Cooking temperature	**high**
Cooking time	**4½–6½ hours**
Serves	**4**
Heat rating	

2 teaspoons peeled and finely grated **root ginger**

4 teaspoons finely grated **garlic**

1 teaspoon **ground cinnamon**

25 g (1 oz) finely chopped **coriander leaves**, plus extra to garnish

875 g (1¾ lb) **minced chicken**

3 tablespoons **sunflower oil**

1 **onion**, finely chopped

2 tablespoons **medium curry powder**

400 g (13 oz) **tinned chopped tomatoes**

200 ml (7 fl oz) **chicken stock**

250 ml (8 fl oz) **single cream**

salt and **pepper**

Creamy kofta curry

Put the ginger, garlic, cinnamon, coriander leaves and minced chicken in a bowl. Season well with salt and pepper. Using your fingers, mix well to combine. Roll tablespoons of the mixture into bite-sized balls, place on a tray, cover and chill for 1–2 hours.

Heat the oil in a large nonstick frying pan over a medium-high heat. Add the rolled chicken balls and cook in batches, frying for about 5 minutes until lightly browned. Remove with a slotted spoon and set aside to keep warm.

Place the onion, curry powder, tomatoes, stock and cream in the slow cooker pot and stir to mix well. Add the browned chicken balls to the pot in a single layer, and stir gently to coat with the sauce. Cover with the lid and cook for 4–6 hours or until cooked through.

Preparation time	**10 minutes, plus marinating**
Cooking temperature	**high**
Cooking time	**4–6 hours**
Serves	**4**
Heat rating	

Bhoona chicken curry

Put the chicken in a non-reactive bowl or shallow dish. Mix together the marinade ingredients and pour over the chicken. Cover with clingfilm and leave to marinate in the refrigerator for 2 hours.

Transfer the chicken mixture to the slow cooker pot and cover with the lid. Cook for 4–6 hours or until tender.

Before serving, sprinkle over the garam masala and chopped coriander, and stir through. Serve hot with steamed rice.

8 large, **skinless chicken thighs** (bone in)

1 teaspoon **garam masala**

handful of roughly chopped **coriander leaves**

FOR THE MARINADE

125 ml (4 fl oz) **natural yogurt**

juice of 2 **limes**

2 **garlic cloves**, finely chopped

1 teaspoon **ground turmeric**

1 tablespoon **mild chilli powder**

1 teaspoon **crushed cardamom seeds**

1 tablespoon **salt**

2 tablespoons **ground coriander**

3 tablespoons **ground cumin**

Preparation time	**15 minutes, plus marinating**
Cooking temperature	**low**
Cooking time	**6½–8½ hours**
Serves	**4**
Heat rating	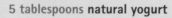

Chicken and spinach curry

5 tablespoons **natural yogurt**

2 tablespoons finely grated **garlic**

2 tablespoons peeled and finely grated **root ginger**

1 tablespoon **ground coriander**

1 tablespoon **curry powder**

750 g (1½ lb) **skinless chicken thigh fillets**, cut into bite-sized pieces

400 g (13 oz) **frozen spinach**, thawed

2 tablespoons **sunflower oil**

1 **onion**, finely chopped

2 teaspoons **cumin seeds**

200 ml (7 fl oz) **water**

1 tablespoon **lemon juice**

salt and **pepper**

Mix together the yogurt, garlic, ginger, coriander and curry powder. Season well with salt and pepper. Put the chicken in a large non-reactive bowl and pour over the yogurt mixture. Toss to mix well, cover and leave to marinate in the refrigerator for 8–10 hours.

Put the spinach in a saucepan and cook over a medium heat for 6–8 minutes. Season with salt and pepper, and drain thoroughly. Transfer to a food processor and blend until smooth.

Heat the oil in a large nonstick frying pan over a low heat. Add the onion and fry gently for 10–12 minutes until soft and translucent. Add the cumin seeds and stir-fry for 1 minute until fragrant. Increase the heat to high, add the chicken mixture and stir-fry for 6–8 minutes.

Transfer the chicken mixture to the slow cooker pot. Pour in the measurement water and the spinach purée. Stir to mix well. Cover with the lid and cook for 6–8 hours or until the chicken is cooked through.

Stir in the lemon juice and serve immediately.

Preparation time	**10 minutes**
Cooking temperature	**low**
Cooking time	**6½–8½ hours**
Serves	**4**
Heat rating	🌶

125 ml (4 fl oz) **cider vinegar**

100–125 ml (3½–4 fl oz) **light soy sauce**

500 ml (17 fl oz) **chicken stock**

2 **bay leaves**

1 teaspoon **pepper**

2 tablespoons **vegetable oil**

1 kg (2 lb) **chicken thighs**

15–20 **garlic cloves,** roughly chopped

Filipino chicken adobo

Put the vinegar, soy sauce, stock, bay leaves and pepper in a saucepan. Bring to the boil, cover and reduce the heat to low. Gently simmer for 15–20 minutes – this forms the adobo stock.

Meanwhile, heat the oil in a large heavy flameproof casserole over a medium-high heat. Add the chicken and brown on all sides for about 5 minutes. Add the garlic and stir-fry for 3–4 minutes, taking care not to let the garlic burn.

Transfer the chicken mixture to the slow cooker pot and add the adobo stock. Cover with the lid and cook for 6–8 hours or until the chicken is cooked through.

Remove the bay leaves and serve with steamed rice.

Preparation time	**5 minutes**
Cooking temperature	**low**
Cooking time	**6–8 hours**
Serves	**4**
Heat rating	🌶🌶

Mandalay chicken curry

Put the curry paste in the slow cooker pot and add the chicken, bamboo shoots, oil, turmeric, shrimp paste and coconut cream. Pour over enough water to cover the chicken and stir to mix well.

Cover with the lid and cook for 6–8 hours or until the chicken is tender and cooked through.

Check the seasoning, adding salt and pepper as needed, and serve hot with rice and lime wedges for squeezing over.

2 tablespoons **medium curry paste**

4 large skinless **chicken breast fillets**, cut into bite-sized cubes

400 g (13 oz) **tinned bamboo shoots**, rinsed and drained

1 tablespoon **sunflower oil**

1 teaspoon **ground turmeric**

1 teaspoon **shrimp paste**

4 tablespoons **coconut cream**

salt and **pepper**

lime wedges, to serve

Preparation time	15 minutes
Cooking temperature	low
Cooking time	6¼–8¼ hours
Serves	4
Heat rating	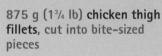

Burmese chicken & prawn curry

875 g (1¾ lb) **chicken thigh fillets**, cut into bite-sized pieces

2 large **onions**, roughly chopped

5 **garlic cloves**, roughly chopped

1 teaspoon peeled and finely grated **root ginger**

2 tablespoons **sunflower oil**

½ teaspoon **Burmese shrimp paste** (belacan)

400 ml (14 fl oz) **coconut milk**

2 tablespoons **medium curry powder**

200 g (7 oz) raw **tiger prawns**, peeled and deveined

salt and **pepper**

TO GARNISH

chopped **coriander leaves**

sliced **red chillies**

lime wedges

Season the chicken pieces with salt and pepper and set aside.

Put the onions, garlic and ginger in a food processor, and blend to a smooth paste (add a little water if needed).

Heat the oil in a large frying pan or saucepan over a high heat. Add the onion mixture and shrimp paste and cook, stirring, for about 5 minutes. Reduce the heat to medium and add the chicken. Cook for about 5 minutes, turning, until the chicken has lightly browned.

Transfer this mixture to the slow cooker pot. Add the coconut milk and curry powder. Cover with the lid and cook for 6–8 hours.

Two hours before the end of the cooking time, stir in the prawns and cook until the prawns are pink and cooked through and the chicken is tender.

Transfer the curry to a serving dish and garnish with chopped coriander, sliced red chillies and lime wedges.

Serve immediately with rice noodles.

Preparation time	**15 minutes**
Cooking temperature	**low**
Cooking time	**6¼–8¼ hours**
Serves	**4**
Heat rating	🌶🌶🌶

400 ml (14 fl oz) **coconut milk**

200 ml (7 fl oz) **coconut cream**

4 large **duck breasts**, cut into bite-sized pieces

2 tablespoons **vegetable oil**

4 tablespoons **Thai red curry paste**

1 tablespoon **palm** or soft **brown sugar**

3 tablespoons **fish sauce** such as nam pla

400 g (13 oz) **tinned bamboo shoots**, drained

200 g (7 oz) **green beans**, halved

4 **kaffir lime leaves**

2 **lemon grass stalks**, lightly bruised

6 tablespoons finely chopped **coriander leaves**, to garnish

Thai duck &
bamboo shoot curry

Pour the coconut milk and half the coconut cream into the slow cooker pot with the duck breasts.

Place the remaining coconut cream in a frying pan or wok over a medium heat. Add the oil and curry paste and stir regularly for 3–4 minutes until the oil starts to separate. Add the sugar and cook for a further 1–2 minutes.

Remove from the heat and pour over the duck mixture in the slow cooker pot along with the fish sauce, bamboo shoots, green beans, kaffir lime leaves and lemon grass. Cover with the lid and cook for 6–8 hours or until the duck is tender.

Scatter with the coriander leaves and serve immediately with cooked jasmine rice.

Preparation time	**10 minutes**
Cooking temperature	**low**
Cooking time	**6¼–8¼ hours**
Serves	4
Heat rating	🌶🌶

Trivandrum
chicken & coconut curry

Heat the oil in a large wok or saucepan over a low heat. Add the onions and fry gently for 10–12 minutes until golden. Add the chillies, garlic, ginger, cassia bark or cinnamon, cardamom, ground coriander, cumin, turmeric and garam masala. Stir-fry for 1 minute until fragrant. Add the chicken and stir-fry over a high heat for 2–3 minutes.

Transfer this mixture to the slow cooker pot. Stir in the tomatoes, sugar and coconut milk, and season with salt. Cover with the lid and cook for 6–8 hours or until the chicken is tender and the sauce has thickened slightly.

Serve immediately with basmati rice.

2 tablespoons **sunflower oil**

2 **onions**, finely chopped

1–2 **red chillies**, deseeded
4 **garlic cloves**, finely grated or crushed

2 teaspoons peeled and finely grated **root ginger**

2 **cassia bark** or **cinnamon sticks**

1 teaspoon **crushed cardamom seeds**

1 tablespoon **ground coriander**

2 teaspoons **ground cumin**

½ teaspoon **ground turmeric**

1 teaspoon **garam masala**

500 g (1 lb) **skinless chicken thigh fillets**, cut into bite-sized pieces

400 g (13 oz) **tinned chopped tomatoes**

2 teaspoons **palm** or **soft brown sugar**

400 ml (14 fl oz) **coconut milk**

salt

Fish & Shellfish

Preparation time	**5 minutes**
Cooking temperature	**high**
Cooking time	**2¼–3¼ hours**
Serves	4
Heat rating	🌶🌶

2 tablespoons **vegetable oil**

2 teaspoons **black mustard seeds**

4 **garlic cloves**, minced

1 teaspoon peeled and finely grated **root ginger**

1 tablespoon **curry powder**

400 g (13 oz) **tinned chopped tomatoes**

¼ teaspoon **sugar**

200 ml (7 fl oz) **water**

200 g (7 oz) **baby spinach leaves**, roughly chopped

750 g (1½ lb) **scallops**, with or without roe

4 tablespoons **double cream**

salt and **pepper**

Scallop & spinach curry

Heat the oil in a large frying pan over a high heat. Add the mustard seeds and, as soon as they start to pop (this won't take long), add the garlic, ginger, curry powder, tomatoes, sugar and measurement water.

Transfer this mixture to the slow cooker pot. Add the spinach and scallops, and cover with the lid. Cook for 2–3 hours until the scallops are cooked through.

Remove from the heat and stir in the cream. Season well with salt and pepper, and serve immediately.

Preparation time	**10 minutes**
Cooking temperature	**high**
Cooking time	**2¼–3¼ hours**
Serves	**4**
Heat rating	🌶🌶🌶

Madras fish curry

Heat the oil in a wide saucepan or frying pan over a medium heat. Add the curry powder and stir-fry for 1–2 minutes until fragrant. Add the mackerel pieces, coriander and red onions, and stir-fry for 20–30 seconds.

Transfer this mixture to the slow cooker pot. Stir in the lime zest and juice, and pour in the coconut milk. Cover with the lid and cook for 2–3 hours or until the fish is cooked through.

Serve immediately with rice and poppadums.

1 tablespoon **vegetable oil**

2 tablespoons **Madras curry powder**

4 large **mackerel**, cleaned and gutted, each cut across into 4 or 5 pieces

small bunch of **coriander**, leaves picked and finely chopped

2 **red onions**, finely chopped

finely grated zest and juice of 1 **lime**

400 ml (14 fl oz) **coconut milk**

Preparation time	**15 minutes**
Cooking temperature	**high**
Cooking time	**2–3 hours**
Serves	4
Heat rating	🌶🌶

4 **garlic cloves**, minced

2 teaspoons peeled and finely grated **root ginger**

2 tablespoons **ground coriander**

1 tablespoon **paprika**

2 teaspoons **ground cumin**

1 teaspoon **hot chilli powder**

½ teaspoon **ground turmeric**

1 tablespoon **jaggery** or **palm sugar**

200 ml (7 fl oz) **water**

1 **mango**, peeled, sliced and stone discarded

400 ml (14 fl oz) **coconut milk**

2 teaspoons **salt**

1 tablespoon **tamarind paste**

1 kg (2 lb) large unpeeled **raw prawns**, heads and tails on

chopped **coriander leaves**, to garnish

Prawn & mango curry

In a bowl, mix together the garlic, ginger, ground coriander, paprika, cumin, chilli powder, turmeric and jaggery or palm sugar. Add the measurement water and stir to mix well.

Transfer to the slow cooker pot. Stir in the mango, coconut milk, salt, tamarind paste and prawns. Cover with the lid and cook for 2–3 hours or until the prawns have turned pink and are cooked through.

Garnish with chopped coriander and serve hot with steamed white rice and a salad of chopped cucumber, tomato and onion.

Preparation time	15 minutes
Cooking temperature	high
Cooking time	2–3 hours
Serves	4
Heat rating	🌶🌶🌶

Thai-style mussel curry

Sort through the mussels, discarding any that have cracked or broken shells. Tap each mussel lightly on the work surface and discard any that don't close.

Heat a wok over a high heat and add the oil. When the oil is hot, add the garlic, ginger, green curry paste, chillies and spring onions. Stir-fry for 30 seconds.

Transfer this mixture to the slow cooker pot. Add the mussels and pour over the coconut milk. Add the lemon grass, soy sauce, lime zest and juice, and sugar. Cover with the lid and cook for 2–3 hours or until all the mussels have opened. Discard any that remain closed.

Remove from the heat and stir in the chopped coriander. Season well with salt and pepper, and serve in warm bowls.

1.5 kg (3 lb) **mussels**, well scrubbed and beards removed

1 tablespoon **sunflower oil**

6 **garlic cloves**, roughly chopped

1 tablespoon peeled and finely chopped **root ginger**

1 teaspoon **Thai green curry paste**

3–4 large **red chillies**, split in half lengthways

6 **spring onions**, finely chopped

400 ml (14 fl oz) **coconut milk**

2 stalks **lemon grass**, tough outer leaves removed, halved lengthways

3 tablespoons **light soy sauce**

finely grated zest and juice of 2 **limes**

1 teaspoon **caster sugar**

large handful of chopped **coriander leaves**

salt and **pepper**

Preparation time	**30 minutes**
Cooking temperature	**high**
Cooking time	**2–3 hours**
Serves	**4**
Heat rating	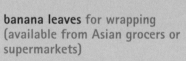

Steamed banana leaf fish

banana leaves for wrapping (available from Asian grocers or supermarkets)

2 teaspoons **ground cumin**

2 teaspoons **ground coriander**

1½ teaspoon **golden caster sugar**

150 g (5 oz) freshly grated **coconut**

4 **green chillies**, deseeded and chopped

8–10 tablespoons chopped **coriander leaves**

4 tablespoons chopped **mint leaves**

5 **garlic cloves**, chopped

1 teaspoon peeled and finely grated **root ginger**

3 tablespoons **vegetable oil**

4 thick **cod fillets**, about 200 g (7 oz) each, skinned

juice of 2 **limes**

salt

Cut the banana leaves into four 24 cm (9¹/₂ inch) squares and soften the banana leaves by dipping them into a pan of very hot water for a few seconds. Wipe the squares dry with kitchen paper as they become pliant.

Using a mortar and pestle or a blender, grind the cumin, ground coriander, sugar, coconut, chillies, fresh coriander, mint, garlic and ginger to a paste. Heat 1 tablespoon of the oil in a frying pan over a low heat and cook the paste, stirring, until aromatic. Season with salt and remove from the heat.

Arrange the banana leaf squares on a work surface. Apply the paste liberally to both sides of each piece of fish. Drizzle the lime juice and remaining oil over the fish. Place a piece of fish on each banana leaf and wrap up like a parcel, securing the parcels with bamboo skewers or string.

Place the parcels in the slow cooker pot, cover with the lid and cook for 2–3 hours or until the fish is cooked through.

Serve hot with rice.

Preparation time	**10 minutes, plus soaking**
Cooking temperature	**high**
Cooking time	**2¼–3¼ hours**
Serves	**4**
Heat rating	♪♪♪

4 **dried chillies**, soaked in hot water for 30 minutes

1 tablespoon **paprika**

3 tablespoons **curry powder**

150 g (5 oz) **freshly grated coconut**

200 ml (7 fl oz) **coconut milk**

4 **mackerel fillets**, 175–250 g (6–8 oz) each, cleaned and gutted

100 ml (3½ fl oz) **water**

2 tablespoons **tamarind paste**

2 **green chillies**, halved lengthways

2.5 cm (1 inch) piece of **root ginger**, peeled and grated

1 small **onion**, finely chopped

salt

Allepy fish curry

Put the soaked chillies, paprika, curry powder and coconut in a blender or food processor. Add the coconut milk and blend to a smooth paste.

Tip the spice paste into a wide, heavy pan. Add the measurement water, stir to mix well and bring to a gentle simmer over a medium-low heat. Add the tamarind paste, green chillies, ginger and onion, and season with salt. Stir and simmer for 2–3 minutes.

Place the mackerel in the slow cooker pot and pour over the spice mixture. Cover with the lid and cook for 2–3 hours or until the mackerel is just cooked.

Serve hot with steamed rice.

Preparation time	10 minutes
Cooking temperature	high
Cooking time	2¼–3¼ hours
Serves	4
Heat rating	🌶

Cochin fish curry

In a small bowl, mix together the turmeric, chilli powder and coconut.

Heat the oil in a large saucepan over a medium heat. When the oil is hot, throw in the mustard seeds and curry leaves. Let these pop and splutter for 1–2 minutes, then add the onion, chillies, ginger and garlic. Stir-fry for about 5 minutes until golden and fragrant. Sprinkle in the turmeric mixture and fry for another 1–2 minutes.

Add the onion mixture to the slow cooker pot and lay the fish on top. Stir in the coconut milk and the measurement water. Finally, stir in the tamarind paste. Cover with the lid and cook for 2–3 hours or until the fish is cooked through.

Season well with salt and serve hot with basmati rice.

1 teaspoon **ground turmeric**

1 tablespoon **chilli powder**

2 tablespoons **freshly grated coconut**

4 tablespoons **vegetable oil**

1 teaspoon **mustard seeds**

20 **curry leaves**

2 **onions**, thinly sliced

4 **green chillies**, deseeded and sliced

2.5 cm (1 inch) piece of **root ginger**, peeled and cut into matchsticks

6 **garlic cloves**, finely chopped

1 kg (2 lb) **pomfret** or **halibut fillets**, skinned and cut into large pieces

400 ml (14 fl oz) **coconut milk**

150 ml (¼ pint) **water**

1 tablespoon **tamarind paste**

salt

Preparation time	**15 minutes**
Cooking temperature	**high**
Cooking time	**2–3 hours**
Serves	**4**
Heat rating	

Bangkok pineapple & prawn curry

2 tablespoons finely chopped **lemon grass**

2 **red chillies**, finely sliced

1 tablespoon peeled and finely grated **root ginger**

½ **onion**, finely chopped

4 **garlic cloves**, crushed

1 teaspoon **ground turmeric**

1 teaspoon **ground coriander**

3 **kaffir lime leaves**, finely shredded

1 tablespoon **palm sugar**

1 tablespoon **fish sauce** such as nam pla

juice of 1 **lime**

400 ml (14 fl oz) **coconut milk**

24 raw **tiger prawns**, peeled and deveined

200 g (7 oz) **pineapple flesh**, cut into bite-sized cubes

100 g (3½ oz) **cherry tomatoes**

6 tablespoons roughly chopped **coriander leaves**

Put the lemon grass, chillies, ginger, onion, garlic, turmeric, ground coriander, kaffir lime leaves, palm sugar, fish sauce and lime juice in a food processor. Add the coconut milk and blend to a smooth paste.

Transfer this mixture to the slow cooker pot and stir in the prawns, pineapple and cherry tomatoes. Cover with the lid and cook for 2–3 hours or until the prawns turn pink and are cooked through.

Stir in the chopped coriander and serve hot with Thai jasmine rice.

Preparation time	**10 minutes**
Cooking temperature	**high**
Cooking time	**2¼–3¼ hours**
Serves	**4**
Heat rating	🌶🌶

Sri Lankan fish curry

2 tablespoons **vegetable oil**

1 large **onion**, chopped

4 **garlic cloves**, finely chopped

10 **curry leaves**

1 teaspoon **ground turmeric**

2 tablespoons **medium curry powder**

2 **tomatoes**, roughly chopped

1 tablespoon **tamarind paste**

400 ml (14 fl oz) **coconut milk**

875 g (1¾ lb) thick **white fish fillets**, skinned and cut into large bite-sized pieces

salt

Heat the oil in a large frying pan over a medium heat. Add the onion, garlic and curry leaves, and stir-fry over a medium-low heat for 8–10 minutes until the onion is soft and lightly golden. Sprinkle over the turmeric and curry powder, and fry for 1–2 minutes until fragrant.

Transfer this mixture into the slow cooker pot. Add the tomatoes (including any juices) and tamarind paste, and pour over the coconut milk. Add the fish on top in a single layer. Season with salt and spoon some of the mixture over the top of the fish. Cover with the lid and cook for 2–3 hours or until the fish is cooked through.

Serve immediately with rice.

Preparation time	**15 minutes**
Cooking temperature	**high**
Cooking time	**2–3 hours**
Serves	**4**
Heat rating	

Malaysian scallop curry

1 tablespoon **red chilli powder**

1 teaspoon **ground coriander**

2 teaspoons **ground cumin**

2 **garlic cloves**, crushed

8 small **shallots**, finely chopped

6 tablespoons finely chopped **lemon grass** (remove tough outer leaves first)

1 teaspoon peeled and finely grated **galangal**

1 tablespoon grated **palm sugar**

½ teaspoon **shrimp paste** such as blachan

2 tablespoons finely chopped **raw skinless peanuts**

600 ml (1 pint) **coconut milk**

200 g (7 oz) **sugar snap peas**, trimmed

875 g (1¾ lb) **scallops**, with or without roe attached

TO GARNISH

Thai sweet basil leaves

chopped **roasted peanuts**

finely sliced **red chillies**

Put the chilli powder, ground coriander, cumin, garlic, shallots, lemon grass, galangal, palm sugar, shrimp paste and unroasted peanuts in a blender or food processor. Pour in the coconut milk and blend until fairly smooth.

Transfer the coconut mixture to the slow cooker pot and add the sugar snap peas and scallops. Cover with the lid and cook for 2—3 hours or until the scallops are cooked through.

Garnish with the Thai sweet basil leaves, chopped roasted peanuts and sliced red chillies, and serve immediately .

Preparation time	15 minutes
Cooking temperature	high
Cooking time	2–3 hours
Serves	4
Heat rating	

2 medium-sized **cooked crabs**

3 **onions**, finely chopped

6 **garlic cloves**, finely chopped

1 tablespoon peeled and finely grated **root ginger**

½ teaspoon **fenugreek seeds**

10 **curry leaves**

1 **cinnamon stick**

2 teaspoons **chilli powder**

1 teaspoon **ground turmeric**

400 ml (14 fl oz) **coconut milk**

salt and **pepper**

Kerala crab curry

Divide each crab into 4 portions, breaking each body in half and separating the large claws from the body. Leave the legs attached. Place in the base of the slow cooker pot.

Add the onion, garlic, ginger, fenugreek, curry leaves, cinnamon, chilli, turmeric and coconut milk to the crabs in the pot. Season well with salt and pepper. Cover with the lid and cook for 2–3 hours or until the curry is fragrant.

Serve immediately with steamed rice. Provide fingerbowls of warm water and lemon slices to clean your fingers.

Preparation time	10 minutes
Cooking temperature	high
Cooking time	2–3 hours
Serves	4
Heat rating	🌶🌶

Chermoula spiced fish

Arrange the lemon slices in a single layer in the base of the slow cooker pot. Place the fish on top of the lemon slices in a single layer. Season with salt.

Put all the chermoula ingredients in a blender or food processor and blend until smooth. Spoon the marinade over the fish, coating the fillets evenly. Cover with the lid and cook for 2–3 hours or until the fish is cooked through.

Serve immediately with couscous or steamed rice.

4 **lemons**, thickly sliced

4 thick **halibut** or **cod fillets**, about 200 g (7 oz) each, skinned

salt

FOR THE CHERMOULA
large bunch of **coriander**, leaves picked and roughly chopped

4 **garlic cloves**, minced

1 teaspoon **ground cumin**

1 teaspoon **ground paprika**

1 teaspoon **chilli powder**

100 ml (3½ fl oz) **extra virgin olive oil**

3 tablespoons **white wine vinegar**

Preparation time	**15 minutes**
Cooking temperature	**high**
Cooking time	**2¼–3¼ hours**
Serves	4
Heat rating	🌶🌶

Masala fennel prawns

1 tablespoon **vegetable oil**

10—12 **curry leaves**

2 large **shallots**, halved and finely sliced

2 teaspoons finely grated **garlic**

1 teaspoon peeled and finely grated **root ginger**

1 tablespoon **fennel seeds**

1 tablespoon **curry powder**

5 large ripe **tomatoes**, deseeded and chopped

750 g (1½ lb) **raw tiger prawns**, peeled and deveined, but tails left intact

salt

Heat the oil in a large wok or nonstick frying pan over a medium heat. Add the curry leaves and stir-fry for 30 seconds before adding the shallots. Stir-fry for a further 4—5 minutes.

Transfer the shallot mixture to the slow cooker pot. Add the garlic, ginger and fennel seeds, sprinkle over the curry powder, and tip in the tomatoes (including any juices). Add the prawns, cover with the lid and cook for 2—3 hours or until the prawns turn pink and are just cooked through.

Season lightly with salt if needed and serve immediately with steamed rice.

Preparation time	**15 minutes, plus marinating**
Cooking temperature	**high**
Cooking time	**2–3 hours**
Serves	**4**
Heat rating	

Halibut & tomato curry

50 ml (2 fl oz) **lemon juice**

50 ml (2 fl oz) **rice wine vinegar**

2 tablespoons **cumin seeds**

2 tablespoons **curry powder**

1 teaspoon **salt**

875 g (1¾ lb) thick **halibut fillets**, skinned and cut into large bite-sized cubes

1 **onion**, finely chopped

3 **garlic cloves**, finely chopped

2 teaspoons peeled and finely grated **root ginger**

400 g (13 oz) **tinned chopped tomatoes**

1 teaspoon **sugar**

Mix together the lemon juice, vinegar, cumin seeds, curry powder and salt in a shallow non-reactive bowl. Add the halibut and turn to coat evenly. Cover and leave to marinate in the refrigerator for 25–30 minutes.

Add the onion, garlic, ginger, tomatoes and sugar to the slow cooker pot, and stir to mix well. Add the halibut and its marinade, and stir gently to mix. Cover with the lid and cook for 2–3 hours or until the halibut is cooked through and flakes easily.

Serve in shallow bowls with rice or noodles.

Preparation time	**15 minutes**
Cooking temperature	**high**
Cooking time	**2–3 hours**
Serves	**4**
Heat rating	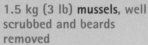

Jamaican jerk mussel curry

1.5 kg (3 lb) **mussels**, well scrubbed and beards removed

6 **spring onions**, roughly chopped

2 **garlic cloves**, crushed

1 **Scotch bonnet chilli**, chopped

1 tablespoon **thyme leaves**

1 tablespoon **curry powder**

finely grated zest and juice of 1 **lime**

4 tablespoons **vegetable oil**

200 g (7 oz) **tinned chopped tomatoes**

lemon wedges, to serve

Sort through the mussels, discarding any that have cracked or broken shells. Tap each mussel lightly on the work surface and discard any that don't close.

Put the spring onions, garlic, chilli, thyme, curry powder, lime zest and juice, and oil in a food processor, and blend to a rough paste. Loosen the mixture by adding a little more oil if needed.

Heat a large wok over a medium-high heat until smoking. Add the paste and fry for 1–2 minutes until fragrant.

Transfer this mixture to the slow cooker pot. Tip in the prepared mussels and the tomatoes. Cover with the lid and cook for 2–3 hours or until all the mussels have opened. Discard any mussels that remain closed.

Serve immediately in a large warm bowl with lemon wedges for squeezing over.

Preparation time	**10 minutes, plus marinating**
Cooking temperature	**high**
Cooking time	**2¼–3¼ hours**
Serves	**4**
Heat rating	

625 g (1¼ lb) **raw king prawns**, peeled and deveined, but with tails left intact

juice of 1 **lime**

1 teaspoon **salt**

1 tablespoon **vegetable oil**

1 small **onion**, finely chopped

2 **garlic cloves**, finely chopped

1 cm (½ inch) piece of **root ginger**, peeled and finely chopped

1 teaspoon **cayenne pepper**

1 teaspoon **paprika**

2 teaspoons **tomato purée**

1 teaspoon **caster sugar**

chopped **coriander leaves**, to garnish

Spicy king prawns

Put the prawns in a bowl and add the lime juice and salt. Leave to marinate in the refrigerator for 30 minutes. Drain, reserving the juices.

Heat the oil in a large frying pan over a low heat and gently fry the onion, garlic and ginger for 10–12 minutes until very soft.

Transfer to the slow cooker pot. Add the prawns, cayenne, paprika, tomato purée and sugar, and stir to mix well. Season and cover with the lid. Cook for 2–3 hours or until the prawns turn pink and are cooked through.

Garnish with coriander leaves and serve immediately.

Preparation time	**15 minutes**
Cooking temperature	**high**
Cooking time	**2¼–3¼ hours**
Serves	**4**
Heat rating	🌶🌶

Fish mollee

Put the onion, garlic, chillies, cumin, ground coriander, turmeric, fresh coriander and the measurement water in a food processor and blend to a smooth paste.

Heat the oil in a large heavy frying pan over a high heat. Add the curry leaves and stir-fry for 20–30 seconds. Add the blended paste and cook, stirring, over a high heat for 3–4 minutes until fragrant.

Transfer this mixture to the slow cooker pot. Add the coconut milk and halibut to the pot in a single layer, and cover with the lid. Cook for 2–3 hours or until the halibut is cooked through.

Garnish with the deep-fried curry leaves and coriander leaves, and serve with steamed basmati rice.

1 **onion**, coarsely grated

4 **garlic cloves**, crushed

2 **green chillies**, deseeded and finely chopped

1 tablespoon **ground cumin**

1 teaspoon **ground coriander**

1 teaspoon **ground turmeric**

25 g (1 oz) **coriander**, finely chopped

200 ml (7 fl oz) **water**

2 tablespoons **sunflower oil**

6 **curry leaves**

400 ml (14 fl oz) **coconut milk**

4 thick **halibut fillets**, 200–250 g (7–8 oz) each, skinned

salt and **pepper**

deep-fried curry leaves and **coriander leaves**, to garnish

Preparation time	**15 minutes**
Cooking temperature	**high**
Cooking time	**2¼–3¼ hours**
Serves	4
Heat rating	

Balinese yellow fish curry

3 **garlic cloves**, finely grated

2 **green chillies**, deseeded and finely chopped

2 teaspoons peeled and finely grated **root ginger**

2 tablespoons **sunflower oil**

1 **onion**, finely chopped

1 tablespoon **ground turmeric**

200 ml (7 fl oz) **coconut milk**

200 ml (7 fl oz) **water**

2 **potatoes**, peeled and cut into small bite-sized pieces

875 g (1¾ lb) thick **cod fillets**, skinned and cut into large bite-sized pieces

2 **tomatoes**, roughly chopped

salt

chopped **coriander leaves**, to garnish

Using a small mortar and pestle, pound the garlic, chillies and ginger into a smooth paste.

Heat the oil in a large nonstick wok or saucepan over a medium heat. Add the paste and stir-fry for 2–3 minutes. Add the onion and turmeric, and stir-fry for a further 2–3 minutes until fragrant.

Transfer this mixture to the slow cooker pot. Stir in the coconut milk and the measurement water, and add the potatoes. Season the cod with salt and add to the pot with the tomatoes. Cover with the lid and cook for 2–3 hours or until the cod is cooked through.

Garnish with coriander leaves and serve hot with steamed white rice.

Preparation time	**10 minutes, plus soaking**
Cooking temperature	**high**
Cooking time	**2¼–3¼ hours**
Serves	**4**
Heat rating	

1 teaspoon **fenugreek seeds**

500 g (1 lb) firm **white fish fillets**, skinned and cut into large bite-sized pieces

1 teaspoon **ground turmeric**

2 teaspoons **salt**

3 **onions**, finely sliced

2 **garlic cloves**, finely chopped

8 **curry leaves**

400 ml (14 fl oz) **coconut milk**

lemon juice, to taste

salt and **pepper**

White fish curry

Soak the fenugreek seeds in water for 30 minutes, then drain.

Pat dry the fish fillets with kitchen paper, then rub them all over with the turmeric and salt, and set aside.

Put the drained fenugreek seeds in a saucepan with the onions, garlic, curry leaves and coconut milk, and season well with salt and pepper. Gently simmer for 12–15 minutes until the onions are soft.

Transfer this mixture to the slow cooker pot and add the fish. Cover with the lid and cook for 2–3 hours or until cooked through.

Add lemon juice to taste and serve immediately with rice and pickles, if liked.

Preparation time	**15 minutes**
Cooking temperature	**high**
Cooking time	**2¼–3¼ hours**
Serves	**4**
Heat rating	🌶🌶🌶

Chettinad pepper prawns

Heat the oil in a large pan over a medium heat. Add the chillies, peppercorns and fennel or star anise, and stir-fry for 1–2 minutes. Increase the heat to high, and add the shallots, garlic and tomato purée. Season with salt and stir to mix well.

Transfer the mixture to the slow cooker pot. Add the prawns and pour in the measurement water. Cover with the lid and cook for 2–3 hours or until the prawns are pink and opaque.

Stir in the green peppercorns and serve immediately.

2 tablespoons **vegetable oil**

3 **dried red chillies**, roughly crushed

1 teaspoon **crushed black peppercorns**

1 teaspoon **crushed fennel seeds** or **star anise**

10 small **shallots**, finely chopped

4 **garlic cloves**, minced

2 tablespoons **tomato purée**

875 g (1¾ lb) **raw king** or **tiger prawns**, peeled and deveined

200 ml (7 fl oz) **water**

2 tablespoons **green peppercorns in brine**, drained

salt

Preparation time	10 minutes
Cooking temperature	high
Cooking time	2–3 hours
Serves	4
Heat rating	

Hot & sour Thai fish curry

2 **garlic cloves**

5 **dried red chillies**

1 teaspoon **salt**

1 teaspoon **ground turmeric**

2 tablespoons finely chopped **lemon grass** (remove tough outer leaves first)

40 g (1½ oz) **shrimp paste**

1 tablespoon **fish sauce** such as nam pla

1 teaspoon **palm sugar**

2 **lemon grass stalks**

600 ml (1 pint) **water**

2 tablespoons freshly squeezed **lemon juice**

1 tablespoon **tamarind paste**

200 g (7 oz) **pineapple**, cut into small bite-sized pieces

4 **salmon fillets**, about 200 g (7 oz) each, skinned

In a blender or small food processor, blend the garlic, chillies, salt, turmeric, lemon grass and shrimp paste until smooth, adding a little water if needed.

Transfer the paste to the slow cooker pot and add the fish sauce and palm sugar. Bruise the lemon grass stalks and add to the pot with two-thirds of the water.

In a small bowl, mix together the lemon juice, tamarind paste and remaining water. Add to the pot with the pineapple and stir to mix well. Add the salmon fillets in a single layer, cover with the lid and cook for 2–3 hours or until the fish is cooked through.

Serve in warm shallow bowls or plates with Thai jasmine rice.

Preparation time	**15 minutes**
Cooking temperature	**high**
Cooking time	**2¼–3¼ hours**
Serves	**4**
Heat rating	

1.5 kg (3 lb) **mussels**, well scrubbed and beards removed

4 tablespoons **vegetable oil**

2 **shallots**, very finely chopped

1 **red chilli**, slit lengthways and deseeded

3 cm (1¼ inch) piece of **root ginger**, peeled and cut into thin shreds

2 **garlic cloves**, peeled and cut into thin shreds

2 **plum tomatoes**, finely chopped

1 tablespoon **curry powder**

200 ml (7 fl oz) **coconut milk**

large handful of chopped **coriander leaves**

3 tablespoons **grated fresh coconut**, to garnish

Spiced mussel curry

Sort through the mussels, discarding any that have cracked or broken shells. Tap each mussel lightly on the work surface and discard any that don't close.

Heat the oil in a saucepan over a medium heat. Add the shallots, chilli, ginger and garlic, and stir-fry for 3–4 minutes.

Transfer this mixture to the slow cooker pot. Add the tomatoes, curry powder, coconut milk and the prepared mussels. Stir to mix well, cover with the lid and cook for 2–3 hours or until all the mussels have opened. Discard any that remain closed.

Stir in the chopped coriander and sprinkle over the grated coconut. Serve immediately with a fresh salad.

Preparation time	**10 minutes**
Cooking temperature	**high**
Cooking time	**2–3 hours**
Serves	4
Heat rating	

Colombo-style coriander prawns

500 g (1 lb) medium **raw prawns**, peeled and deveined

1 tablespoon **medium curry powder**

1 teaspoon **shrimp powder**

4 **garlic cloves**, crushed

2 **shallots**, grated

25 g (1 oz) finely chopped **coriander leaves**

400 ml (14 fl oz) **coconut milk**

4 tablespoons **rice flour**

salt and **pepper**

Using a sharp knife, slit the prawns lengthways along the back and place in the slow cooker pot.

In a separate bowl, mix together the curry powder, shrimp powder, garlic, shallots, coriander, coconut milk and rice flour. Season well with salt and pepper. Stir this mixture into the prawns to mix well.

Cover with the lid and cook for 2–3 hours or until they turn pink and are cooked through.

Serve immediately with steamed white rice and pickles, if liked.

Preparation time	**15 minutes, plus marinating**
Cooking temperature	**high**
Cooking time	**2$\frac{1}{2}$–3$\frac{1}{2}$ hours**
Serves	**4**
Heat rating	

Tamarind fish curry

1 tablespoon **tamarind paste**

50 ml (2 fl oz) **rice wine vinegar**

2 tablespoons **cumin seeds**

1 teaspoon **ground turmeric**

1 teaspoon **chilli powder**

1 teaspoon **salt**

750 g (1$\frac{1}{2}$ lb) thick **cod fillets**, skinned and cut into large bite-sized cubes

4 tablespoons **sunflower oil**

1 **onion**, finely chopped

3 **garlic cloves**, finely grated

2 tablespoons peeled and finely grated **root ginger**

2 teaspoons **black mustard seeds**

875 g (1$\frac{3}{4}$ lb) **tinned chopped tomatoes**

1 teaspoon **sugar**

In a shallow non-reactive bowl, mix together the tamarind, vinegar, cumin, turmeric, chilli powder and salt. Add the cod and turn to coat evenly. Cover and leave to marinate in the refrigerator for 25–30 minutes.

Meanwhile, heat a wok over a high heat and add the oil. When the oil is hot, add the onion, garlic, ginger and mustard seeds. Reduce the heat and cook gently for 10 minutes, stirring occasionally.

Add the tomatoes and sugar, stir through and bring to the boil. Reduce the heat again, cover and cook gently for 15–20 minutes, stirring occasionally.

Transfer this mixture to the slow cooker pot. Add the cod and its marinade in a single layer and stir gently to mix. Cover with the lid and cook for 2–3 hours or until the cod is cooked through and flakes easily.

Serve in shallow bowls with steamed basmati rice and poppadums.

Preparation time	**10 minutes**
Cooking temperature	**high**
Cooking time	**2¼–3¼ hours**
Serves	**4**
Heat rating	

2 tablespoons **vegetable oil**

2 **onions**, finely chopped

2 tablespoons **curry powder**

1 teaspoon **ground turmeric**

1 kg (2 lb) **monkfish tail fillets**, skinned and cut into large bite-sized pieces

2 **garlic cloves**, chopped

1 teaspoon peeled and finely grated **root ginger**

½ teaspoon **tamarind paste**

1 tablespoon **thyme leaves**

1 **star anise**

450 ml (¾ pint) **fish stock**

Seychelles monkfish curry

Heat the oil in a heavy pan over a low heat, and fry the onions for 8–10 minutes until lightly golden. Stir in the curry powder and turmeric, and fry for a further 1 minute until fragrant.

Transfer this mixture to the slow cooker pot. Add the pieces of monkfish and all the other ingredients. Cover with the lid and cook for 2–3 hours or until the monkfish is cooked through.

Serve hot with rice.

Preparation time	**15 minutes**
Cooking temperature	**high**
Cooking time	**2–3 hours**
Serves	4
Heat rating	🌶 🌶 🌶

Malabari spiced prawns

Put the curry powder, tamarind paste, chilli powder, cumin and turmeric in a small bowl. Add 4 tablespoons of the water and stir to mix well. Set aside.

Place the garlic and prawns in the slow cooker pot. Stir in the ginger, chilli slices and the curry and tamarind mixture, and pour over the remaining water. Cover with the lid and cook for 2–3 hours or until the prawns turn pink and are just cooked through.

Season with salt and stir in the coriander. Serve immediately with basmati rice, naan bread and chutney, if liked.

1 tablespoon **curry powder**

1 teaspoon **tamarind paste**

1 teaspoon **hot chilli powder**

2 teaspoons **ground cumin**

1 teaspoon **ground turmeric**

150 ml (¼ pint) **water**

3 **garlic cloves**, finely chopped

16 large **raw tiger** or **king prawns**, peeled and deveined, but with tail left intact

1 teaspoon peeled and finely grated **root ginger**

1 **red chilli**, finely sliced

100 ml (3½ fl oz) **coconut milk**

6 tablespoons finely chopped **coriander leaves**

salt

Preparation time	**10 minutes**
Cooking temperature	**high**
Cooking time	**2¼–3¼ hours**
Serves	**4**
Heat rating	🌶🌶

Thai fish ball curry

1 tablespoon **sunflower oil**

1 tablespoon **Thai red curry paste**

600 ml (1 pint) **coconut milk**

500 g (1 lb) **cooked fish balls** (available in all major Thai grocers or Oriental supermarkets)

2 teaspoons finely grated **palm sugar**

4 **kaffir lime leaves**, finely shredded

1 tablespoon very finely chopped **lemon grass** (remove tough outer leaves first)

2 teaspoons **fish sauce** such as nam pla

1 **carrot**, cut into thin matchsticks

150 g (5 oz) **mangetout**, halved lengthways

TO GARNISH

sliced **red chilli**

coriander leaves

Heat the oil in a large nonstick wok over a medium heat and add the curry paste. Stir-fry for 1–2 minutes, then add the coconut milk. Bring to the boil, reduce the heat to low and simmer gently, uncovered, for 6–8 minutes.

Transfer this mixture to the slow cooker pot. Add the fish balls, palm sugar, kaffir lime leaves, lemon grass, fish sauce, carrot and mangetout. Cover with the lid and cook for 2–3 hours or until the fish balls and vegetables are cooked through.

Garnish with sliced red chilli and coriander leaves, and serve in warm bowls with steamed jasmine rice.

Preparation time	**5 minutes**
Cooking temperature	**high**
Cooking time	**2¼–3¼ hours**
Serves	**4**
Heat rating	

2 tablespoons **butter**

1 **onion**, finely chopped

2 **garlic cloves**, finely chopped

2 tablespoons **curry powder**

2 **spring onions**, finely sliced

2 large **tomatoes**, finely chopped

1 kg (2 lb) **cooked lobster meat**, roughly chopped

2 teaspoons **cornflour**

200 ml (7 fl oz) **cold water**

Caribbean lobster curry

Melt the butter in a large frying pan over a medium heat. Add the onion, garlic, curry powder, spring onions and tomatoes, and stir-fry for 6–8 minutes. Add the lobster and stir-fry for a further 6–8 minutes.

Transfer the lobster mixture to the slow cooker pot. Mix the cornflour with the measurement water and add to the pot. Stir to mix well, cover with the lid and cook for 2–3 hours or until the sauce has thickened and the lobster is cooked through.

Serve hot with white rice.

Preparation time	**5 minutes**
Cooking temperature	**high**
Cooking time	**2¼–3¼ hours**
Serves	4
Heat rating	🌶🌶🌶

Spiced prawn & pineapple curry

Heat half the oil in a large wok over a medium heat. Add the aubergine and stir-fry for 5–6 minutes. Add the remaining oil and the curry paste and stir-fry for a further 3–4 minutes until fragrant.

Transfer this mixture to the slow cooker pot. Pour over the coconut milk and add the pineapple, pineapple juice, chillies and prawns. Cover with the lid and cook for 2–3 hours or until the prawns have turned pink and are cooked through.

Season with the fish sauce and serve immediately.

4 tablespoons **vegetable oil**

1 **aubergine**, cut into bite-sized cubes

1 tablespoon **Thai green curry paste**

400 ml (14 fl oz) **coconut milk**

300 g (10 oz) **pineapple flesh**, cut into bite-sized cubes

3 tablespoons **pineapple juice**

2–3 **green chillies**, left whole

875 g (1¾ lb) unpeeled **raw tiger prawns**

1 tablespoon **fish sauce** such as nam pla

Preparation time	15 minutes
Cooking temperature	high
Cooking time	2¼–3¼ hours
Serves	4
Heat rating	🌶🌶🌶

Vietnamese fish curry

400 ml (14 fl oz) **coconut cream**

100 ml (3½ fl oz) **water**

6 **kaffir lime leaves**

300 g (10 oz) peeled and deveined **raw tiger prawns**

400 g (13 oz) firm **salmon fillets**, skinned and cut into bite-sized pieces

20 **Thai sweet basil leaves**

4 tablespoons finely chopped **coriander leaves**

6 **spring onions**, finely chopped

FOR THE CURRY PASTE

1 tablespoon **sunflower oil**

4 **shallots**, finely chopped

4 **garlic cloves**, crushed

2 tablespoons finely chopped **lemon grass** (remove tough outer leaves first)

1 tablespoon peeled and finely grated **root ginger**

1 tablespoon **curry powder**

1 teaspoon **ground cinnamon**

6 **star anise**

To make the curry paste, heat the oil in a wok or heavy frying pan over a medium-high heat. Add the shallots, garlic, lemon grass and ginger, and fry for 3—4 minutes. Add the dried spices and cook for a couple of minutes, stirring occasionally, until the spices are toasted and very aromatic.

Pour the coconut cream and the measurement water into the slow cooker pot, and add the kaffir lime leaves and curry paste mixture. Stir in the prawns and salmon pieces. Cover with the lid and cook for 2—3 hours or until the prawns and fish are cooked through.

Stir in the chopped Thai basil, coriander and spring onions, and serve immediately with steamed rice.

Preparation time	10 minutes
Cooking temperature	high
Cooking time	2¼–3¼ hours
Serves	4
Heat rating	🌶 🌶 🌶

2 tablespoons **vegetable oil**

1 **onion**, finely chopped

2 **garlic cloves**, crushed

1 **Scotch bonnet chilli**, deseeded and finely chopped

1 tablespoon **thyme leaves**

1 tablespoon **mild curry powder**

1 **red pepper**, halved lengthways, deseeded and cut into small bite-sized pieces

6 **spring onions**, finely sliced

200 g (7 oz) **tinned chopped tomatoes**

400 ml (14 fl oz) **coconut milk**

500 g (1 lb) **crayfish meat**

salt and **pepper**

Tobago crayfish curry

Heat the oil in a large heavy frying pan over a medium heat. Add the onion, garlic, chilli and thyme, and sauté for about 5 minutes until the onion is soft.

Stir in the curry powder and cook for 1 minute until fragrant. Add the red pepper, spring onions and tomatoes, and cook for a further 1 minute.

Transfer this mixture to the slow cooker pot. Pour in the coconut milk and stir in the crayfish. Cover with the lid and cook for 2–3 hours or until the crayfish turns pink and is cooked through.

Serve with steamed rice.

Preparation time	**20 minutes**
Cooking temperature	**high**
Cooking time	**2¼–3¼ hours**
Serves	**4**
Heat rating	🌶🌶

Achari prawns

Heat the oil in a large nonstick wok or frying pan over a medium heat. Add the shallots and stir-fry for 10 minutes until lightly golden. Add the curry leaves, garlic, ginger and chillies, and stir-fry for 1 minute. Add the ground coriander and the cumin, mustard, nigella and fennel seeds. Season well with salt and pepper, and stir-fry for 1–2 minutes until fragrant.

Transfer this mixture into the slow cooker pot. Stir in the tomatoes and the prawns. Cover with the lid and cook for 2–3 hours or until the prawns turn pink and opaque.

Stir in the chopped coriander and serve immediately.

4 tablespoons **sunflower oil**

8 **shallots**, finely chopped

6–8 **curry leaves**

1 tablespoon finely grated **garlic**

1 tablespoon peeled and finely grated **root ginger**

3 **red chillies**, halved lengthways

1 tablespoon **ground coriander**

2 teaspoons **cumin seeds**

2 teaspoons **black mustard seeds**

2 teaspoons **nigella seeds**

2 teaspoons **fennel seeds**

400 g (13 oz) **tinned chopped tomatoes**

875 g (1¾ lb) small **raw prawns**, peeled and deveined

6 tablespoons finely chopped **coriander leaves**

salt and **pepper**

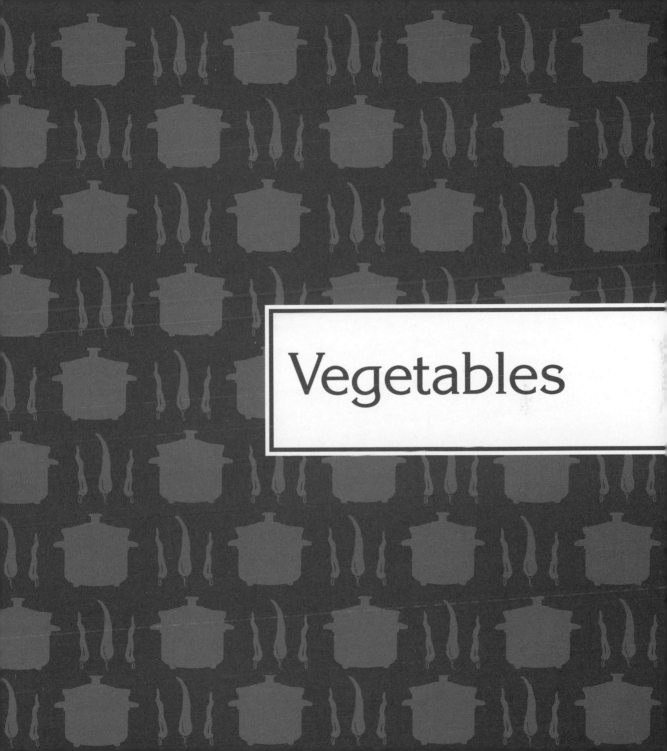

Vegetables

Preparation time	**5 minutes**
Cooking temperature	**high**
Cooking time	**4¼–6¼ hours**
Serves	**4**
Heat rating	🌶🌶

4 tablespoons **sunflower oil**

1–2 teaspoons **black mustard seeds**

1 teaspoon **coarse chilli powder** or **paprika**

4 teaspoons **cumin seeds**

8–10 **curry leaves**

2 teaspoons **ground cumin**

2 teaspoons **ground coriander**

1 teaspoon **ground turmeric**

500 g (1 lb) peeled and boiled **potatoes**, cut into 2.5 cm (1 inch) cubes

250 ml (8 fl oz) **boiling water**

6 tablespoons chopped **coriander leaves**

squeeze of **lemon juice**

salt and **pepper**

Bombay aloo

Heat the oil in a large nonstick wok or frying pan over a medium-high heat. Add the mustard seeds, chilli powder or paprika, cumin seeds and curry leaves. Stir-fry for 1–2 minutes until fragrant.

Transfer this mixture to the slow cooker pot. Add the ground spices and potatoes. Season well with salt and pepper, and stir in the measurement boiling water. Cover with the lid and cook for 4–6 hours or until most of the liquid is absorbed.

Stir in the coriander and squeeze over the lemon juice before serving hot.

Preparation time	15 minutes
Cooking temperature	high
Cooking time	4¼–6¼ hours
Serves	4
Heat rating	🌶🌶

Mushroom & tomato curry

Put the garlic, ginger, onion, curry powder and measurement water in a blender or food processor, and blend until smooth.

Heat 3 tablespoons of the oil in a large nonstick wok over a high heat. Add the mushrooms and stir-fry for 4–5 minutes. Transfer the contents of the wok to the slow cooker pot and wipe out the wok with kitchen paper. Heat the remaining oil in the wok over a medium heat. Add the onion mixture and stir-fry for 3–4 minutes.

Transfer the onion mixture to the slow cooker pot with the coconut milk and tomatoes. Season well with salt and pepper. Cover with the lid and cook for 4–6 hours or until the mushrooms are tender.

Stir in the chopped coriander and serve immediately.

4 **garlic cloves**, finely chopped

2 teaspoons peeled and finely chopped **root ginger**

1 **onion**, finely chopped

1 tablespoon **curry powder**

3 tablespoons **water**

75 ml (3 fl oz) **sunflower oil**

500 g (1 lb) large **button mushrooms**, halved or thickly sliced

100 ml (3½ fl oz) **coconut milk**

4 **tomatoes**, finely chopped

6 tablespoons finely chopped **coriander leaves**

salt and **pepper**

Preparation time	**10 minutes**
Cooking temperature	**low**
Cooking time	**6–8 hours**
Serves	4
Heat rating	🌶🌶

1 **pandanus leaf**

600 ml (1 pint) **coconut milk**

1 **onion**, chopped

1 tablespoon peeled and finely grated **root ginger**

1 teaspoon peeled and finely grated **galangal**

2 **green chillies**, deseeded and finely chopped

8 **curry leaves**

1 **cinnamon stick**

1 teaspoon **ground turmeric**

250 g (8 oz) **raw cashew nuts**

2 tablespoons chopped **coriander leaves**, to garnish

Cashew nut curry

Shred the pandanus leaf lengthways into about three sections and tie into a large knot.

Put the coconut milk, onion, ginger, galangal, chillies, curry leaves, cinnamon stick, turmeric, cashew nuts and pandanus leaf into the slow cooker pot. Cover with the lid and cook for 6–8 hours or until the nuts are tender.

Discard the galangal, cinnamon stick and pandanus leaf. Sprinkle over the coriander leaves and serve hot with rice and pickles, if liked.

Preparation time	**20 minutes**
Cooking temperature	**low**
Cooking time	**6¼–8¼ hours**
Serves	**4**
Heat rating	

Paneer & pea curry

Heat the oil in a large nonstick wok over a medium-high heat. Add the shallots and stir-fry for 2–3 minutes. Sprinkle over the curry powder and stir-fry for a further 1 minute until fragrant.

Transfer this mixture to the slow cooker pot. Add the tomatoes, garlic, chillies, tomato purée, sugar, cream, paneer, peas and the measurement water. Cover with the lid and cook for 6–8 hours or until the paneer is heated through and the peas are cooked.

Season well with salt and pepper and stir in the chopped coriander just before serving.

2 tablespoons **sunflower oil**

8 **shallots**, finely chopped

2 tablespoons **curry powder**

4 ripe **plum tomatoes**, roughly chopped

2 teaspoons finely grated **garlic**

2 **red chillies**, deseeded and finely sliced

2 tablespoons **tomato purée**

1 teaspoon **sugar**

200 ml (7 fl oz) **single cream**

450 g (14½ oz) **paneer (Indian cottage cheese)**, cut into bite-sized pieces

200 g (7 oz) **frozen peas**

150 ml (¼ pint) **water**

6 tablespoons finely chopped **coriander leaves**

salt and **pepper**

Preparation time	**15 minutes**
Cooking temperature	**low**
Cooking time	**6¼–8¼ hours**
Serves	**4**
Heat rating	🌶

Moroccan spiced vegetable tagine

2 tablespoons **sunflower oil**

1 large **onion**, finely chopped

2 **garlic cloves**, minced

1 teaspoon peeled and finely grated **root ginger**

2 teaspoons **ground cumin**

1 teaspoon **ground coriander**

2 teaspoons **ground cinnamon**

1 teaspoon **ground turmeric**

1 teaspoon **dried red chilli flakes**

400 g (13 oz) **tinned chopped tomatoes**

250 ml (8 fl oz) **vegetable stock**

400 g (13 oz) **tinned chickpeas**, rinsed and drained

200 g (7 oz) **green beans**, halved

1 **red pepper**, halved lengthways, deseeded and cut into small bite-sized pieces

750 g (1½ lb) **butternut squash**, peeled, deseeded and cut into bite-sized cubes

100 g (3½ oz) **golden raisins** or **sultanas**

salt and **pepper**

Heat the oil in a large nonstick frying pan over a medium heat. Add the onion and stir-fry for 4–5 minutes. Add the garlic, ginger, cumin, coriander, cinnamon, turmeric, chilli flakes and tomatoes, and stir-fry for 4–5 minutes.

Transfer this mixture to the slow cooker pot. Stir in the stock, chickpeas, green beans, red pepper, butternut squash and raisins or sultanas. Cover with the lid and cook for 6–8 hours or until the vegetables are cooked through and tender.

Season with salt and pepper and serve with couscous or rice.

Preparation time	**20 minutes**
Cooking temperature	**low**
Cooking time	**6¼–8¼ hours**
Serves	**4**
Heat rating	🌶 🌶 🌶

3 firm ripe **mangoes**, peeled, stoned and cut into small bite-sized pieces

1 teaspoon **ground turmeric**

1 teaspoon **chilli powder**

500 ml (17 fl oz) **water**

325 g (11 oz) **freshly grated coconut**

3–4 **green chillies**, roughly chopped

1 tablespoon **cumin seeds**

300 ml (½ pint) **coconut milk**

4 tablespoons **vegetable oil**

2 teaspoons **black mustard seeds**

3–4 **hot dried red chillies**

10–12 **curry leaves**

South Indian mango curry

Put the mangoes in a heavy saucepan. Add the turmeric, chilli powder and half the measurement water. Bring to the boil, remove from the heat and transfer to the slow cooker pot.

In a food processor, blend the coconut, green chillies and cumin seeds with the remaining water to make a fine paste.

Add the coconut paste to the mango mixture with the coconut milk. Stir to mix well, cover with the lid and cook for 6–8 hours or until the mixture has thickened slightly.

Heat the oil in a small pan over a medium-high heat. When hot, add the mustard seeds. When the mustard seeds begin to pop, add the dried chillies and curry leaves. Stir-fry for a few seconds until the chillies darken. Pour the oil mixture into the mango curry and serve immediately.

Preparation time	**5 minutes**
Cooking temperature	**low**
Cooking time	**6½–8½ hours**
Serves	**4**
Heat rating	

Lebanese courgette curry

Heat the oil in a large saucepan over a low heat. Add the onion and fry for 10–12 minutes until soft and translucent. Add the courgettes and cook for a further 5–6 minutes, stirring occasionally.

Transfer this mixture to the slow cooker pot. Tip in the tomatoes (including any juices) and garlic, and stir in the chilli powder, turmeric and mint. Cover with the lid and cook for 6–8 hours or until the mixture has thickened slightly.

Season well with salt and pepper and serve with steamed basmati rice.

2 tablespoons **olive oil**

1 large **onion**, finely chopped

4 large **courgettes**, cut into 1 cm (½ inch) cubes

875 g (1¾ lb) **tinned peeled whole plum tomatoes**

2 **garlic cloves**, crushed

½ teaspoon **chilli powder**

¼ teaspoon **ground turmeric**

1 teaspoon **dried mint**

salt and **pepper**

Preparation time	10 minutes
Cooking temperature	low
Cooking time	6–8 hours
Serves	4
Heat rating	🌶🌶

Sweet potato curry

1 **onion**, chopped

3 **garlic cloves**, minced

2 **red chillies**, finely chopped

1 teaspoon **ground turmeric**

1 teaspoon peeled and finely grated **root ginger**

1 tablespoon **light soy sauce**

250 ml (8 fl oz) **coconut milk**

1 tablespoon **lemon juice**

450 g (14½ oz) **sweet potatoes**, peeled and cut into 2 cm (¾ inch) cubes

200 ml (7 fl oz) **boiling water**

small handful of chopped **coriander leaves**

Put the onion, garlic, chillies, turmeric, ginger, soy sauce, coconut milk, lemon juice and sweet potatoes into the slow cooker pot. Pour over the measurement boiling water, cover with the lid and cook for 6–8 hours or until the sweet potatoes are tender.

Stir in the coriander leaves and serve immediately with rice.

Preparation time	**10 minutes**
Cooking temperature	**low**
Cooking time	**6¼–8¼ hours**
Serves	4
Heat rating	🌶🌶

Creamy butternut squash curry

Put the butternut squash in a saucepan of boiling water and cook for about 5–6 minutes until slightly softened. Drain and place in the slow cooker pot.

Add the green curry paste and pour over the coconut milk. Add the lime zest and juice and soy sauce, and stir to mix well. Cover with the lid and cook for 6–8 hours or until the squash is tender.

Serve hot with jasmine rice.

1 large **butternut squash**, halved, deseeded and peeled, and cut into 2 cm (¾ inch) cubes

1 tablespoon **Thai green curry paste**

400 ml (14 fl oz) **coconut milk**

finely grated zest and juice of 1 **lime**

1 tablespoon **light soy sauce**

Preparation time	**15 minutes**
Cooking temperature	**low**
Cooking time	**6¼–8¼ hours**
Serves	**4**
Heat rating	

Goan xacutti curry

3 **potatoes**, peeled and chopped into 2.5 cm (1 inch) cubes

2 large **carrots**, chopped into 2.5 cm (1 inch) cubes

400 g (13 oz) **tinned chopped tomatoes**

250 ml (8 fl oz) **boiling water**

200 g (7 oz) **frozen peas**

salt

FOR THE XACUTTI CURRY PASTE

2 teaspoons **vegetable oil**

3 **whole cloves**

2 **cinnamon sticks**

2 teaspoons **white poppy seeds**

2 teaspoons **whole black peppercorns**

4 **dried red chillies**

75 g (3 oz) **desiccated coconut**

4 **garlic cloves**, roughly chopped

2 **onions**, roughly chopped

First make the curry paste. Heat the oil in a small frying pan over a medium heat. Add the cloves, cinnamon, poppy seeds, peppercorns and dried chillies, and fry for 1–2 minutes until fragrant.

In a separate pan, dry-roast the coconut over a medium-low heat for a few minutes until golden brown. Put the roasted coconut, fried spices, garlic and onions in a blender or food processor, and grind to a paste.

Place the potatoes and carrots in the slow cooker pot with the curry paste and chopped tomatoes, and season with salt. Pour over the measurement boiling water and stir well. Cover with the lid and cook for 6–8 hours or until the potatoes, peas and carrots are tender.

Serve hot with steamed rice.

Preparation time	**15 minutes**
Cooking temperature	**high**
Cooking time	**4¼–6¼ hours**
Serves	4
Heat rating	🌶🌶

4 tablespoons **sunflower oil**

1 **onion**, finely chopped

1 tablespoon **black mustard seeds**

1 tablespoon **cumin seeds**

2–3 **dried red chillies**

10–12 **curry leaves**

625 g (1¼ lb) **okra**, cut diagonally into 1.5 cm (¾ inch) lengths

½ teaspoon **ground turmeric**

200 ml (7 fl oz) **boiling water**

100 g (3½ oz) **freshly grated coconut**

salt and **pepper**

Spiced okra curry

Heat the oil in a wok over a medium heat. Add the onion and stir-fry for 5–6 minutes until soft and translucent. Add the mustard seeds, cumin seeds, chillies and curry leaves, and stir-fry over a high heat for 2 minutes until fragrant.

Transfer this mixture to the slow cooker pot. Stir in the okra and turmeric, and pour over the measurement boiling water. Cover with the lid and cook for 4–6 hours or until the okra is very soft and tender.

Sprinkle over the coconut and season well with salt and pepper. Serve immediately with steamed rice.

Preparation time	15 minutes
Cooking temperature	low
Cooking time	6¼–8¼ hours
Serves	4
Heat rating	

Beetroot curry

Heat the oil in a wok or saucepan over a medium heat. Add the mustard seeds. As soon as they begin to pop (a matter of seconds), add the onion, garlic and chillies, and fry for about 5 minutes until the onion is soft and translucent. Add the remaining spices and the beetroot, and fry for a further 1–2 minutes.

Transfer to the slow cooker pot. Add the tomatoes, measurement water and a pinch of salt. Cover and cook for 6–8 hours or until the beetroot is tender.

Stir in the coconut cream and lime juice, and check the seasoning. Garnish with some chopped coriander and serve immediately.

2 tablespoons **vegetable oil**

1 teaspoon **black mustard seeds**

1 **onion**, chopped

2 **garlic cloves**, chopped

2 **red chillies**, deseeded and finely chopped

8 **curry leaves**

1 teaspoon **ground turmeric**

1 teaspoon **cumin seeds**

1 **cinnamon stick**

400 g (13 oz) **raw beetroot**, peeled and cut into matchsticks

200 g (7 oz) **tinned chopped tomatoes**

250 ml (8 fl oz) **water**

50 ml (2 fl oz) **coconut cream**

juice of 1 **lime**

salt

chopped **coriander leaves**, to garnish

Preparation time	**20 minutes**
Cooking temperature	**high**
Cooking time	**4¼–6¼ hours**
Serves	**4**
Heat rating	🌶🌶

Indian spinach & cottage cheese curry

500 g (1 lb) **frozen spinach**

60 g (2 oz) **ghee** or **butter**

2 teaspoons **cumin seeds**

1 **onion**, very finely chopped

2 **plum tomatoes**, finely chopped

2 teaspoons finely grated **garlic**

1 tablespoon peeled and finely grated **root ginger**

1 teaspoon **chilli powder**

1 teaspoon **ground coriander**

250 g (8 oz) **paneer (Indian cottage cheese)**, cut into bite-sized pieces

2 tablespoons **double cream**

1 teaspoon **lemon juice**

2 tablespoons finely chopped **coriander leaves**

salt and **pepper**

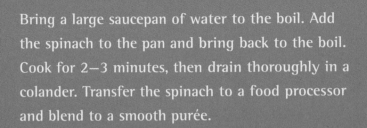

Bring a large saucepan of water to the boil. Add the spinach to the pan and bring back to the boil. Cook for 2–3 minutes, then drain thoroughly in a colander. Transfer the spinach to a food processor and blend to a smooth purée.

Meanwhile, heat the ghee or butter in a large heavy frying pan over a medium-low heat. Add the cumin seeds and onion, and stir-fry for 6–8 minutes until the onion is lightly golden.

Transfer this mixture to the slow cooker pot with the spinach. Add the tomatoes, garlic, ginger, chilli powder and ground coriander. Place the paneer in this mixture and season well with salt and pepper. Cover with the lid and cook for 4–6 hours or until the mixture has thickened.

Stir in the cream, lemon juice and chopped coriander. Serve immediately with warm naan bread or rice.

Preparation time	**10 minutes**
Cooking temperature	**low**
Cooking time	**6¼–8¼ hours**
Serves	**4**
Heat rating	

2 tablespoons **vegetable oil**

8–10 **garlic cloves**, minced

4 cm (1¾ inch) piece of **root ginger**, peeled and thinly sliced

10 **whole black peppercorns**

1 **green papaya**, peeled, deseeded and thinly sliced

300 ml (½ pint) **coconut milk**

100 ml (3½ fl oz) **boiling water**

200 ml (7 fl oz) **coconut cream**

salt

Filipino green papaya curry

Heat the oil in a large wok or saucepan over a medium heat. Add the garlic and fry for a few minutes until lightly golden. Add the ginger and peppercorns and fry for a further 3–4 minutes.

Transfer this mixture to the slow cooker pot. Add the papaya, pour over the coconut milk and the measurement boiling water, and season well with salt. Cover with the lid and cook for 6–8 hours or until the papaya is translucent.

Stir in the coconut cream and serve immediately.

Preparation time	**10 minutes**
Cooking temperature	**low**
Cooking time	**6¼–8¼ hours**
Serves	**4**
Heat rating	🌶

Cauliflower curry

Heat the oil in a large nonstick frying pan over a medium heat. Add the spring onions and stir-fry for 2–3 minutes. Add the garlic, ginger and curry powder, and stir-fry for 20–30 seconds until fragrant. Add the cauliflower and red and green peppers, and stir-fry for a further 2–3 minutes.

Transfer this mixture to the slow cooker pot. Stir in the tomatoes and chickpeas, and season well with salt and pepper. Cover with the lid and cook for 6–8 hours or until the vegetables are tender.

Drizzle with the yogurt, garnish with the chopped mint and serve hot with steamed rice.

2 tablespoons **vegetable oil**

8 **spring onions**, cut into 5 cm (2 inch) lengths

2 teaspoons grated **garlic**

2 teaspoons **ground ginger**

2 tablespoons **curry powder**

300 g (10 oz) **cauliflower florets**

1 **red pepper**, halved lengthways, deseeded and cut into bite-sized cubes

1 **green pepper**, halved lengthways, deseeded and cut into bite-sized cubes

400 g (13 oz) **tinned chopped tomatoes**

200 g (7 oz) **tinned chickpeas**, rinsed and drained

3–4 tablespoons **natural yogurt**

salt and **pepper**

large handful of chopped **mint leaves**, to garnish

Preparation time	**20 minutes**
Cooking temperature	**low**
Cooking time	**6¼–8¼ hours**
Serves	**4**
Heat rating	_ _ _

Thai red pumpkin curry

2 tablespoons **sunflower oil**

1 **red onion,** halved and thinly sliced

2 **garlic cloves,** minced

1 teaspoon peeled and finely grated **root ginger**

3 tablespoons **Thai red curry paste**

875 g (1¾ lb) (prepared weight) **pumpkin,** peeled, deseeded and cut into bite-sized cubes

400 ml (14 fl oz) **coconut milk**

200 ml (7 fl oz) **boiling water**

6 **kaffir lime leaves**

2 teaspoons grated **palm sugar**

3 **lemon grass stalks,** bruised

salt and **pepper**

TO GARNISH

small handful of **Thai sweet basil leaves**

50 g (2 oz) **skinless raw peanuts,** roasted and roughly chopped

Heat the oil in a large nonstick wok or frying pan over a medium heat. Add the onion, garlic and ginger, and stir-fry for 3−4 minutes. Stir in the curry paste and pumpkin and stir-fry for a further 3−4 minutes.

Transfer this mixture to the slow cooker pot. Pour over the coconut milk and the measurement boiling water, and add the lime leaves, palm sugar and lemon grass. Cover with the lid and cook for 6−8 hours or until the pumpkin is tender.

Check the seasoning, adding salt and pepper if needed. Scatter over the basil leaves and peanuts, and serve immediately.

Preparation time	**20 minutes**
Cooking temperature	**high**
Cooking time	**4¼–6¼ hours**
Serves	**4**
Heat rating	

3 tablespoons **sunflower oil**

1 teaspoon **black mustard seeds**

3 teaspoons **cumin seeds**

8–10 **curry leaves**

2 teaspoons **ground cumin**

2 teaspoons **ground coriander**

1 teaspoon **ground turmeric**

500 g (1 lb) peeled and boiled **potatoes**, cut into 2.5 cm (1 inch) cubes

200 ml (8 fl oz) **boiling water**

4 tablespoons chopped **coriander leaves**

juice of ½–1 **lime**

salt and **pepper**

Cumin potato curry

Heat the oil in a large nonstick wok or frying pan over a medium-high heat. Add the mustard seeds, cumin seeds and curry leaves, and stir-fry for 1–2 minutes until fragrant.

Transfer this mixture to the slow cooker pot. Add the ground spices and potatoes. Season well with salt and pepper, and pour over the measurement boiling water. Cover with the lid and cook for 4–6 hours or until the potatoes are tender.

Stir in the coriander and squeeze over the lime juice. Serve immediately with naan bread or rice.

Preparation time	**15 minutes**
Cooking temperature	**low**
Cooking time	**6¼–8¼ hours**
Serves	**4**
Heat rating	🌶🌶

South Indian vegetable curry

Heat the oil in a large heavy frying pan over a medium heat. Add the shallots and stir-fry for 4–5 minutes. Add the mustard seeds, curry leaves, chilli, ginger, turmeric, cumin and peppercorns, and stir-fry for a further 1–2 minutes until fragrant.

Transfer this mixture to the slow cooker pot. Add the carrots, courgette, beans and potato to the pot. Pour over the coconut milk and the vegetable stock or water. Cover with the lid and cook for 6–8 hours or until the vegetables are tender.

Season well with salt and pepper and squeeze over the lemon juice immediately before serving.

2 tablespoons **sunflower oil**

6 **shallots**, halved and thinly sliced

2 teaspoons **black mustard seeds**

8–10 **curry leaves**

1 **green chilli**, thinly sliced

2 teaspoons peeled and finely grated **root ginger**

1 teaspoon **ground turmeric**

2 teaspoons **ground cumin**

6 **whole black peppercorns**

2 **carrots**, cut into thick batons

1 **courgette**, cut into thick batons

200 g (7 oz) **green beans**, trimmed

1 large **potato**, peeled and cut into thick batons

300 ml (½ pint) **coconut milk**

100 ml (3½ fl oz) **vegetable stock** or **water**

juice of ½ **lemon**

salt and **pepper**

Preparation time	**10 minutes, plus soaking**
Cooking temperature	**high**
Cooking time	**4¼–6¼ hours**
Serves	**4**
Heat rating	

Ceylonese pea curry

300 g (10 oz) **cashew nuts**, soaked in cold water for 3 hours

1 teaspoon **turmeric**

1 **lemon grass stalk**

2 tablespoons **vegetable oil**

2 **onions**, halved and sliced

2 **garlic cloves**, chopped

1 **cinnamon stick**

6 **curry leaves**

1 teaspoon **cayenne pepper**

1 teaspoon **paprika**

1 tablespoon **medium curry powder**

150 g (5 oz) **frozen peas**

300 ml (½ pint) **coconut milk**

25 g (1 oz) chopped **coriander leaves**

salt

Drain the soaked cashew nuts, then simmer with the turmeric in lightly salted water for about 30 minutes until soft and creamy. Drain, discarding the cooking liquid.

Meanwhile, trim the top off the lemon grass stalk, leaving just the lower 7–8 cm (3–3½ inches), then lightly bash this with a wooden mallet or rolling pin to bruise slightly (this helps to release the aromatic oils within).

Heat the oil in a saucepan or wok over a medium heat. Add the onions and fry for about 5 minutes. Stir in the garlic, cinnamon stick and curry leaves, and fry for a further 3–4 minutes until the onion is soft and translucent. Sprinkle over the cayenne, paprika and curry powder, and fry for 30–40 seconds until fragrant.

Transfer this mixture to the slow cooker pot along with the cashew nuts and peas. Pour over the coconut milk and add the bruised lemon grass and a pinch of salt. Cover with the lid and cook for 4–6 hours or until the peas are tender.

Sprinkle with the chopped coriander and serve with steamed white rice.

Preparation time	15 minutes
Cooking temperature	low
Cooking time	6¼–8¼ hours
Serves	4
Heat rating	🌶 🌶 🌶

1 tablespoon **vegetable oil**

2 **onions**, finely chopped

1 **red pepper**, halved lengthways, deseeded and finely chopped

6 **spring onions**, finely chopped

3 **garlic cloves**, minced

1 tablespoon finely chopped **thyme leaves**

2 teaspoons **curry powder**

300 ml (½ pint) **boiling water**

2 **carrots**, cut into bite-sized cubes

1 **Scotch bonnet chilli**

500 g (1 lb) **potatoes**, peeled and cut into bite-sized cubes

400 g (13 oz) **tinned chopped tomatoes**

2 **courgettes**, halved lengthways and sliced

West Indian vegetable curry

Heat the oil in a large flameproof casserole over a medium-high heat. Add the onions, red pepper, spring onions, garlic, thyme leaves and curry powder, and stir-fry for 5 minutes.

Transfer this mixture to the slow cooker pot. Pour over the measurement boiling water and add the carrots, chilli, potatoes, tomatoes and courgettes. Cover with the lid and cook for 6–8 hours or until the vegetables are tender.

Discard the Scotch bonnet chilli and serve immediately with rice.

Preparation time	**10 minutes**
Cooking temperature	**high**
Cooking time	**4–6 hours**
Serves	4
Heat rating	🌶🌶

Shredded cabbage curry

Wash the cabbage well, drain and put in a large saucepan (water should still be clinging to the leaves).

Transfer to the slow cooker pot. Add the onion, chillies, turmeric and mustard seeds, and pour over the measurement boiling water. Cover with the lid and cook for 4–6 hours or until the cabbage is tender.

Add the toasted coconut, stir well and serve immediately.

250 g (8 oz) **green cabbage**, very finely shredded

1 **onion**, finely chopped

2 **green chillies**, deseeded and chopped

½ teaspoon **ground turmeric**

1 teaspoon **black mustard seeds**

300 ml (½ pint) **boiling water**

40 g (1½ oz) **desiccated** or **freshly grated coconut**, lightly toasted

Preparation time	20 minutes
Cooking temperature	high
Cooking time	4½–6½ hours
Serves	4
Heat rating	🌶🌶

Nonya laksa

2 tablespoons **vegetable oil**

2 tablespoons finely chopped **garlic**

1 tablespoon finely chopped **lemon grass**
(remove tough outer leaves first)

1 tablespoon peeled and finely chopped **root ginger**

2 **red chillies**, sliced

2 **onions**, finely sliced

4 tablespoons **medium curry powder**

½ teaspoon **ground turmeric**

300 ml (½ pint) **vegetable stock**

400 ml (14 fl oz) **coconut milk**

1 teaspoon **palm sugar**

250 g (8 oz) **dried rice noodles** or **rice sticks**

TO ACCOMPANY

4 **spring onions**, finely sliced

25 g (1 oz) finely chopped **coriander leaves**

3 **hard-boiled eggs**, halved or quartered

100 g (3½ oz) **roasted skinless peanuts**,
roughly chopped

50 g (2 oz) **bean sprouts**

Heat a wok or large frying pan over a high heat. Add the oil and, when it is very hot and slightly smoking, reduce the heat and add the garlic, lemon grass, ginger, chillies and onions. Stir-fry for 1–2 minutes.

Transfer this mixture to the slow cooker pot. Add the curry powder, turmeric and stock. Add the coconut milk and palm sugar, and stir to mix well. Cover with the lid and cook for 4–6 hours.

Meanwhile, soak the rice noodles or rice sticks in a bowl of warm water for 20 minutes or until tender. Drain in a colander or sieve.

Put the rice noodles into 4 warmed, wide bowls and spoon over the laksa sauce. Serve immediately with the accompaniments.

Preparation time	**10 minutes**
Cooking temperature	**high**
Cooking time	**4¼–6¼ hours**
Serves	**4**
Heat rating	

1 tablespoon **vegetable oil**

1 **onion**, sliced

1–2 **hot green chillies**, sliced

1 **garlic clove**, minced

5–6 **curry leaves**

1 tablespoon **curry powder**

¼ teaspoon **ground turmeric**

½ teaspoon **fenugreek seeds**

450 g (14½ oz) **green beans**, trimmed and halved

125 ml (4 fl oz) **coconut milk**

squeeze of **lime juice**

salt and **pepper**

Sri Lankan green bean curry

Heat the oil in a saucepan over a medium heat. Add the onion, chillies, garlic and curry leaves, and fry for 6–8 minutes until the onions are golden brown. Sprinkle over the curry powder, turmeric and fenugreek seeds. Stir through and fry for 2–3 minutes until fragrant.

Transfer this mixture to the slow cooker pot. Add the beans and pour over the coconut milk. Season well with salt and pepper. Cover with the lid and cook for 4–6 hours or until the beans are tender.

Add a squeeze of lime juice and serve immediately with rice or bread.

Preparation time	**15 minutes**
Cooking temperature	**low**
Cooking time	**6¼–8¼ hours**
Serves	**4**
Heat rating	

Cambodian vegetable curry

Heat the oil in a large saucepan over a medium heat. Fry the shallots for a few minutes until soft and translucent. Stir in the garlic, ginger, lemon grass and curry powder and fry gently for a further 5 minutes until fragrant.

Transfer this mixture to the slow cooker pot. Add the red pepper, carrot, mushrooms and tofu, and stir through. Pour over the measurement boiling water, then add the potatoes and coconut milk. Season well with salt and pepper. Cover with the lid and cook for 6–8 hours or until the potatoes and vegetables are tender.

Ladle the curry into large wide bowls, garnish each bowl with a pile of bean sprouts and serve with steamed rice or bread.

1 tablespoon **vegetable oil**

6 **shallots**, roughly chopped

1 **garlic clove**, chopped

4 cm (1½ inch) piece of **root ginger**, peeled and thinly sliced

2 **lemon grass stalks**, tough outer leaves removed, cut into 5 cm (2 inch) pieces

1 tablespoon **curry powder**

1 **red pepper**, halved lengthways, deseeded and roughly chopped

1 **carrot**, cut into diagonal slices

4 **mushrooms**, sliced

225 g (7½ oz) **fried tofu**, cut into bite-sized pieces

250 ml (8 fl oz) **boiling water**

4 small **potatoes**, peeled and quartered

400 ml (14 fl oz) **coconut milk**

salt and **pepper**

50 g (2 oz) **bean sprouts**, to garnish

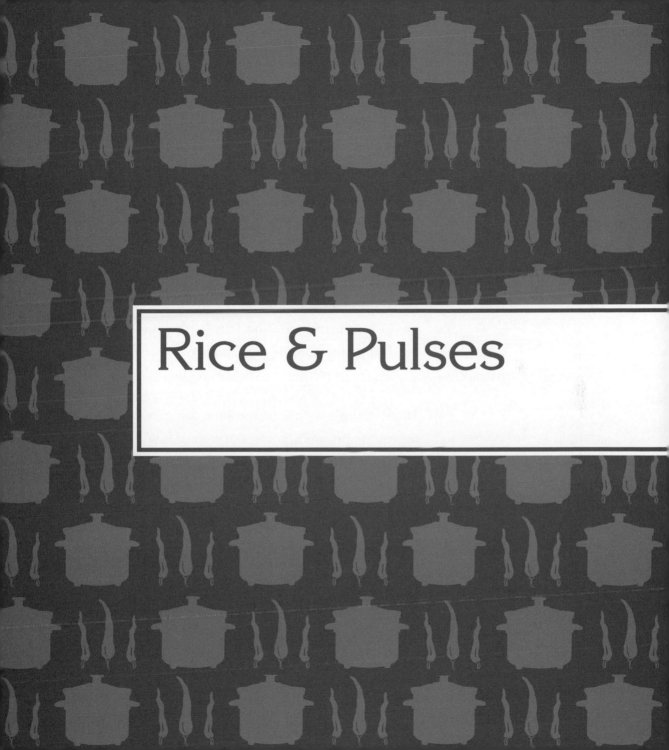

Rice & Pulses

Preparation time	15 minutes
Cooking temperature	**low**
Cooking time	**4¼–6¼ hours**
Serves	4
Heat rating	

1 tablespoon **ghee**

2 **cinnamon sticks**

2 **green cardamom pods**

2–3 **whole cloves**

2 teaspoons **saffron threads**, soaked in 3 tablespoons **warm milk**

¼ teaspoon **ground turmeric**

225 g (7½ oz) **easy-cook basmati rice**, well rinsed and drained

500 ml (17 fl oz) **boiling water**

salt

Saffron rice

Heat the ghee in a nonstick saucepan over a medium heat. When hot, add the cinnamon, cardamom, cloves, saffron mixture and turmeric, and stir-fry for 20–30 seconds until fragrant. Add the rice and cook, stirring, for 2 minutes until the rice grains are well coated.

Transfer this mixture to the slow cooker pot. Pour over the measurement boiling water and season with salt. Cover with the lid and cook for 4–6 hours or until the liquid is absorbed and the rice is tender.

Fluff up the rice grains with a fork and serve immediately with any curry dish.

Preparation time	**15 minutes, plus soaking**
Cooking temperature	**low**
Cooking time	**6¼–8¼ hours**
Serves	**4**
Heat rating	

Tarka dhal

Place the lentils in a bowl and cover with boiling water. Allow to soak for 1 hour and then drain.

Put the drained lentils in the slow cooker pot with the measurement boiling water, turmeric and tomatoes. Cover with the lid and cook for 6–8 hours or until the lentils are tender.

Using a balloon whisk, whisk until the mixture is fairly smooth. Season with salt and pepper, and stir in the chopped coriander.

To make the tarka, heat the oil in a large frying pan over a medium-high heat. When the oil is hot, add all the other ingredients and stir-fry for 1–2 minutes until fragrant. Remove from the heat and pour over the cooked dhal. Stir through and serve immediately with warm naan bread and rice.

250 g (8 oz) **split red lentils**, picked over, rinsed and drained thoroughly

750 ml (1¼ pints) **boiling water**

1 teaspoon **ground turmeric**

4 ripe **tomatoes**, roughly chopped

6–8 tablespoons finely chopped **coriander leaves**

salt and **pepper**

FOR THE TARKA (SPICED OIL)
4 tablespoons **sunflower oil**

2 teaspoons **black mustard seeds**

3 teaspoons **cumin seeds**

2 **garlic cloves**, very thinly sliced

2 teaspoons peeled and very finely chopped **root ginger**

6–8 **curry leaves**

1 whole **dried red chilli**

2 teaspoons **ground cumin**

2 teaspoons **ground coriander**

Preparation time	10 minutes
Cooking temperature	low
Cooking time	4¼–6¼ hours
Serves	4
Heat rating	🌶

2 tablespoons **vegetable oil**

1 large **onion**, finely chopped

2 **garlic cloves**, finely chopped

2 teaspoons **cumin seeds**

2 **cloves**

1 teaspoon **crushed cardamom seeds**

2 **cinnamon sticks**

1 tablespoon **turmeric**

250 g (8 oz) **easy-cook basmati rice**

500 ml (17 fl oz) **boiling water**

20 g (¾ oz) finely chopped **coriander leaves**

salt and **pepper**

Aromatic pilaf rice

Heat the oil in a heavy saucepan over a medium heat. Add the onion and gently fry for 4–5 minutes. Stir in the garlic, cumin, cloves, cardamom, cinnamon and turmeric, and stir-fry for 1–2 minutes until fragrant. Add the rice and mix well.

Transfer this mixture to the slow cooker pot. Pour in the measurement boiling water and season well with salt and pepper. Cover the pan with the lid and cook for 4–6 hours or until the liquid is absorbed and the rice is tender.

Stir in the chopped coriander just before serving.

Preparation time	**20 minutes**
Cooking temperature	**low**
Cooking time	**4¼–6¼ hours**
Serves	4
Heat rating	🌶🌶🌶

Spiced chickpea curry

Heat the oil in the wok over a low heat. Add the onions and cook over a low heat for 15 minutes until lightly golden. Add the ground coriander, cumin, chilli powder, turmeric and curry powder, and stir-fry for 1–2 minutes until fragrant.

Add the tomatoes, sugar and measurement water to the slow cooker pot. Add the chickpeas and onion mixture, and season well with salt and pepper. Cover with the lid and cook for 4–6 hours or until the mixture is thick.

Just before serving, stir in the mint. Divide the spinach leaves among 4 shallow bowls and top with the chickpea mixture. Drizzle over the yogurt and serve immediately with steamed rice or bread.

2 tablespoons **sunflower oil**

2 **onions**, halved and thinly sliced

2 teaspoons **ground coriander**

2 teaspoons **ground cumin**

1 teaspoon **hot chilli powder**

½ teaspoon **ground turmeric**

1 tablespoon **curry powder**

400 g (13 oz) **tinned chopped tomatoes**

1 teaspoon **golden caster sugar**

100 ml (3½ fl oz) **water**

400 g (13 oz) **tinned chickpeas**, rinsed and drained

2 tablespoons chopped **mint leaves**

salt and **pepper**

TO SERVE
100 g (3½ oz) **baby leaf spinach**

100 ml (3½ fl oz) **natural yogurt**, lightly whisked

Preparation time	**15 minutes**
Cooking temperature	**low**
Cooking time	**6¼–8¼ hours**
Serves	**4**
Heat rating	

Chicken & red lentil curry

175 g (6 oz) **split red lentils,** picked over and rinsed

2 tablespoons **vegetable oil**

2 **onions,** finely sliced

2 **garlic cloves,** minced

2 tablespoons **medium curry powder**

1 teaspoon **cumin seeds**

500 g (1 lb) **skinless chicken breast fillets,** thinly sliced

500 ml (17 fl oz) **chicken stock**

100 ml (3½ fl oz) **coconut cream**

50 g (2 oz) **raw cashew nuts**

Place the drained lentils in a bowl and cover with boiling water. Allow to stand for 1 hour and then drain thoroughly.

Heat 1 tablespoon of the oil in a large frying pan over a low heat. Add the onion and gently fry for 8–10 minutes, stirring occasionally, until soft and translucent. Stir in the garlic, curry powder and cumin seeds, and cook for a further 1–2 minutes until fragrant. Add the remaining oil and the chicken, and cook for 2–3 minutes until the chicken is coated in the spice mixture.

Transfer this mixture to the slow cooker pot. Stir in the stock, lentils and coconut cream. Cover with the lid and cook for 6–8 hours or until the chicken is tender.

Meanwhile, heat a small nonstick frying pan over a medium heat and dry-roast the cashew nuts for 2–3 minutes, stirring regularly until golden brown.

Top with the roasted cashews and serve immediately in individual bowls with basmati rice.

Preparation time	**10 minutes**
Cooking temperature	**low**
Cooking time	**4¼–6¼ hours**
Serves	**4**
Heat rating	

Channa masala

4 tablespoons **sunflower oil**

4 **garlic cloves**, minced

2 teaspoons peeled and finely grated **root ginger**

1 large **onion**, coarsely grated

1–2 **green chillies**, finely sliced

1 teaspoon **hot chilli powder**

1 tablespoon **ground cumin**

1 tablespoon **ground coriander**

3 tablespoons **natural yogurt**, plus extra, whisked, to drizzle

2 teaspoons **garam masala**

2 teaspoons **tamarind paste**

2 teaspoons **curry powder**

875 g (1¾ lb) **tinned chickpeas**, rinsed and drained

500 ml (17 fl oz) **boiling water**

chopped **coriander leaves**, to garnish

lemon wedges, to serve

Heat the oil in a large heavy frying pan over a medium heat. Add the garlic, ginger, onion and chillies, and stir-fry for 6–8 minutes until the onion is lightly golden. Add the chilli powder, cumin, ground coriander, yogurt and garam masala, and stir-fry for a further 1–2 minutes.

Transfer the onion mixture to the slow cooker pot. Add the tamarind paste, curry powder and chickpeas. Pour over the measurement boiling water and stir to mix well. Cover with the lid and cook for 4–6 hours or until the sauce is thick and rich.

Garnish with chopped coriander and serve in small bowls, drizzled with a little extra whisked yogurt, and with lemon wedges on the side for squeezing over.

Preparation time	**15 minutes, plus soaking**
Cooking temperature	**low**
Cooking time	**6¼–8¼ hours**
Serves	**4**
Heat rating	

Spiced aubergine dhal

175 g (6 oz) **split yellow lentils**, picked over and rinsed

3 tablespoons **sunflower oil**

2 **onions**, finely chopped

4 **garlic cloves**, finely chopped

1 teaspoon peeled and finely grated **root ginger**

1 tablespoon **cumin seeds**

1 tablespoon **black mustard seeds**

2 tablespoons **curry powder**

600 ml (1 pint) **boiling water**

1 **aubergine**, cut into bite-sized cubes

8 **cherry tomatoes**

25 g (1 oz) chopped **coriander**

salt

Place the rinsed lentils in a bowl and pour over boiling water to cover. Allow to soak for 1 hour and then drain thoroughly.

Heat the oil in a medium saucepan over a high heat. Add the onions and stir-fry for 6–8 minutes until they start to turn golden. Reduce the heat and stir in the garlic, ginger, cumin and mustard seeds and curry powder. Stir-fry for 1–2 minutes until fragrant.

Add the lentils to the slow cooker pot and stir in the onion mixture. Pour over the measurement boiling water. Stir in the aubergine and cherry tomatoes. Cover with the lid and cook for 6–8 hours or until the dhal is thick and the lentils are tender.

Season well with salt and stir in the chopped coriander. Serve immediately with the bread or steamed basmati rice.

Preparation time	**5 minutes**
Cooking temperature	**low**
Cooking time	**4¼–6¼ hours**
Serves	**4**
Heat rating	

4 tablespoons **vegetable oil**

8 **garlic cloves**, thinly sliced

6 **shallots**, halved and thinly sliced

250 g (8 oz) **easy-cook long-grain rice**

600 ml (1 pint) **boiling water**

2 teaspoons **ground turmeric**

1 teaspoon **saffron threads**

salt

Burmese golden rice

Heat the oil in a nonstick frying pan over a medium-low heat and fry the garlic and shallots for 5–6 minutes until lightly browned and crisp. Drain on kitchen paper and set aside.

Put the rice in the slow cooker pot. Add the measurement boiling water and season with salt. Add the turmeric and saffron, and stir well. Cover with the lid and cook for 4–6 hours or until the liquid is absorbed and the rice is tender.

Fluff up the rice grains with a fork and pile onto a platter. Serve immediately, sprinkled with the fried garlic and shallots.

Preparation time	5 minutes, plus soaking
Cooking temperature	**low**
Cooking time	**4¼–6¼ hours**
Serves	**4**
Heat rating	🌶🌶

Coconut & curry leaf rice

Wash the rice in several changes of water, then soak for 15 minutes in a bowl of cold water. Drain thoroughly and transfer to the slow cooker pot.

Heat the ghee in a heavy saucepan over a medium heat. Add the mustard and cumin seeds, chillies and curry leaves, and stir-fry for 30 seconds. Add the measurement boiling water and the coconut cream, and stir to mix well.

Pour this mixture over the rice in the pot. Cover with the lid and cook for 4–6 hours or until the liquid is absorbed and the rice is tender.

Serve with any curry dish.

225 g (7½ oz) **easy-cook basmati rice**

2 tablespoons **ghee**

2 teaspoons **black mustard seeds**

2 teaspoons **cumin seeds**

2 **dried red chillies**, roughly chopped

10 **curry leaves**

500 ml (17 fl oz) **boiling water**

100 ml (3½ fl oz) **coconut cream**

Preparation time	**15 minutes, plus soaking**
Cooking temperature	**low**
Cooking time	**6¼–8¼ hours**
Serves	4
Heat rating	

Sambhar

250 g (8 oz) **split red lentils**, picked over and rinsed

900 ml (1½ pints) **boiling water**

1 teaspoon **ground turmeric**

4 tablespoons **vegetable oil**

2 **dried red chillies**

1 teaspoon **black mustard seeds**

½ teaspoon **fenugreek seeds**

8 **curry leaves**

1 **onion**, finely chopped

4 tablespoons **tamarind paste**, dissolved in 200 ml (7 fl oz) hot water

¼ teaspoon **asafoetida powder**

1 large **tomato**, finely chopped

2 **carrots**, chopped

200 g (7 oz) **green beans**, cut into bite-sized pieces

FOR THE SAMBHAR POWDER

1 teaspoon **ground coriander**

1 teaspoon **red chilli powder**

1 teaspoon **ground cumin**

1 teaspoon **ground black pepper**

½ teaspoon **black mustard seeds**

pinch of **ground cinnamon**

pinch of **ground cloves**

Put the lentils in a deep bowl and cover with boiling water. Leave to soak for 1–2 hours or overnight if time permits. When ready to cook, transfer to a colander and rinse under cold running water.

In a small bowl, mix together all the ingredients for the sambhar powder and set aside.

Put the drained lentils in the slow cooker pot with the measurement boiling water. Add the turmeric and half the oil. Cover with the lid and cook for 6–8 hours or until the lentils are soft, then whisk until it forms a coarse mixture.

Meanwhile, in a separate pan, heat the remaining oil over a medium heat. When the oil is hot, add the chillies, mustard and fenugreek seeds and curry leaves, and fry for 2 minutes until fragrant and the mustard seeds start to pop. Add the onion and continue to fry for about 5 minutes until the onion is lightly browned. Add the tamarind mixture and allow to boil lightly for a few minutes until the onions are completely soft and translucent.

Add the onion mixture to the lentils with the asafoetida, tomato, carrots, beans and sambhar powder. Serve immediately with steamed rice.

Preparation time	40 minutes, plus soaking
Cooking temperature	low
Cooking time	6½–8½ hours
Serves	4
Heat rating	🌶🌶

125 g (4 oz) **dried whole black lentils**, picked over, rinsed and drained thoroughly

1 litre (1¾ pints) **boiling water**

3 tablespoons **butter**

1 **onion**, finely chopped

3 **garlic cloves**, crushed

2 teaspoons peeled and finely grated **root ginger**

2 **green chillies**, split in half lengthways

1 teaspoon **ground turmeric**

1 teaspoon **paprika**, plus extra for sprinkling

1 tablespoon **ground coriander**

1 tablespoon **ground cumin**

200 g (7 oz) **cooked red kidney beans**

large handful of **chopped coriander leaves**

150 ml (¼ pint) **double cream**

salt

Kali dhal

Put the lentils in a deep bowl and cover with cold water. Leave to soak for 10–12 hours. Transfer to a colander and rinse under cold running water. Drain and put in a saucepan with half the measurement boiling water. Bring to the boil and cook for 20 minutes. Drain and set aside.

Melt the butter in a large saucepan over a medium heat. Add the onion, garlic, ginger and chillies, and stir-fry for 5–6 minutes until the onion is soft and translucent. Add the turmeric, paprika, ground coriander, cumin, red kidney beans and reserved lentils, and stir through for a minute or so.

Transfer this mixture to the slow cooker pot and pour over the remaining boiling water. Cover with the lid and cook for 6–8 hours or until the mixture has thickened.

Season with salt, stir in the chopped coriander, drizzle over the cream and sprinkle over a little extra paprika.

Preparation time	**10 minutes, plus soaking**
Cooking temperature	**low**
Cooking time	**4¼–6¼ hours**
Serves	**4**
Heat rating	

Mushroom pilaf

Soak the rice in a bowl of cold water for 20 minutes. Drain thoroughly.

Heat the oil in a heavy saucepan over a high heat. Add the mushrooms and stir-fry for 6–8 minutes. Add the spices and crisp-fried onions or shallots, and stir-fry for 2–3 minutes. Add the peas and stir-fry for a further 2–3 minutes. Add the rice and stir for a minute or so until the grains are well coated.

Transfer to the slow cooker pot. Pour over the measurement boiling water and season well with salt and pepper. Cover with the lid and cook for 4–6 hours or until the liquid is absorbed and the rice is tender.

Fluff up the rice grains with a fork and serve immediately.

275 g (9 oz) **easy-cook basmati rice**, rinsed and drained

4 tablespoons **sunflower oil**

200 g (7 oz) **mushrooms**, sliced

1 **cinnamon stick**

2 teaspoons **cumin seeds**

2 **whole cloves**

4 **green cardamom pods**, lightly bruised

8 **whole black peppercorns**

4 tablespoons **crisp-fried onions** or **shallots** (available from Thai and other Asian grocers)

200 g (7 oz) **frozen peas**

500 ml (17 fl oz) **boiling water**

salt and **pepper**

Preparation time	**30 minutes**
Cooking temperature	**low**
Cooking time	**6½–8½ hours**
Serves	**4**
Heat rating	

Persian lamb & lentil curry

6 tablespoons **red lentils**, picked over and rinsed

6 tablespoons **yellow split peas**

750 g (1½ lb) boned **lamb shoulder** or **leg**, cut into large chunks

300 g (10 oz) **butternut squash**, peeled, deseeded and roughly chopped

200 g (7 oz) **potatoes**, peeled and chopped into chunks

1 teaspoon **ground turmeric**

4 tablespoons **sunflower oil**

2 large **onions**, roughly chopped

2 teaspoons **cumin seeds**

1 tablespoon **ground coriander**

1 teaspoon peeled and finely grated **root ginger**

3 teaspoons finely grated **garlic**

1 tablespoon **medium curry powder**

2 teaspoons **tamarind paste**

2 teaspoons **runny honey**

salt and **pepper**

Place the drained lentils and split peas in a bowl and cover with boiling water. Allow to soak for 1 hour, then drain thoroughly.

Put the lamb, lentils, split peas, butternut squash, potatoes and turmeric in the slow cooker pot. Season well with salt and pepper, and pour over just enough water to cover. Cover with the lid and cook for 6–8 hours or until the meat and vegetables are tender.

Heat 3 tablespoons of the oil in a large frying pan over a low heat. Stir-fry the onions for 15–20 minutes until golden brown. Reserve half the onions and set aside. Add the rest to the lamb mixture.

Heat the remaining oil in the same frying pan over a medium heat. Fry the cumin seeds, coriander, ginger, garlic and curry powder for 2–3 minutes until fragrant. Stir this mixture into the lamb curry along with the tamarind and honey until well mixed.

Garnish with the reserved onions and serve immediately with a vegetable pilaf, mango chutney and crispy poppadums.

Preparation time	**5 minutes**
Cooking temperature	**low**
Cooking time	**4½–6½ hours**
Serves	**4**
Heat rating	

50 g (2 oz) **ghee** or **vegetable oil**

1 **onion**, chopped

300 g (10 oz) **minced chicken**

1 **cinnamon stick**

8 **green cardamom pods**, cracked

3 tablespoons **sultanas**

200 g (7 oz) **easy-cook basmati rice**

large pinch of **saffron threads**

500 ml (17 fl oz) **boiling chicken stock**

100 g (3½ oz) **toasted pine nuts**

salt and **pepper**

Lebanese chicken rice

Heat the ghee or oil in a medium heavy saucepan over a medium-low heat and fry the onion for 10–15 minutes until golden brown and starting to caramelize. Remove with a slotted spoon and set aside.

Using the same pan, stir-fry the minced chicken over a high heat for 4–5 minutes. Add the cinnamon, cardamom, sultanas, rice and saffron. Season well with salt and pepper and stir-fry for 2–3 minutes.

Transfer this mixture to the slow cooker pot. Return the onion mixture to the pot and pour over the boiling stock. Cover with the lid and cook for 4–6 hours or until the liquid is absorbed and the rice is tender.

Sprinkle with the pine nuts and serve warm.

Preparation time	**10 minutes**
Cooking temperature	**low**
Cooking time	**4¼–6¼ hours**
Serves	**4–6**
Heat rating	🌶

Turkish vermicelli & rice pilaf

Heat the butter and oil in a heavy saucepan over a medium heat. When the butter has melted, sauté the vermicelli for a few minutes until golden brown, stirring constantly. Stir in the rice and cook, stirring, for about 1 minute until the grains are well coated.

Transfer this mixture to the slow cooker pot. Add the chicken stock and season with salt and pepper. Cover with the lid and cook for 4–6 hours or until all the liquid is absorbed and the vermicelli and rice are tender.

Fluff up the rice grains with a fork, sprinkle with the cinnamon, cloves and cardamom, and serve warm.

4 tablespoons **butter**

2 tablespoons **olive oil**

200 g (7 oz) **vermicelli**, broken into 2.5 cm (1 inch) lengths

250 g (9 oz) **easy-cook long-grain rice**

500 ml (17 fl oz) **boiling chicken stock**

½ teaspoon **ground cinnamon**

¼ teaspoon **ground cloves**

½ teaspoon **ground cardamom**

salt and **pepper**

Preparation time	**10 minutes, plus soaking**
Cooking temperature	**low**
Cooking time	**6¼–8¼ hours**
Serves	**4**
Heat rating	

Creamy spinach & tomato dhal

200 g (7 oz) **red lentils**, picked over, rinsed and drained thoroughly

400 ml (14 fl oz) **boiling water**

300 ml (½ pint) **coconut milk**

1 teaspoon **ground turmeric**

100 g (3½ oz) **spinach leaves**, roughly chopped

4 **tomatoes**, roughly chopped

small handful of finely chopped **coriander leaves**

2 tablespoons **ghee** or **vegetable oil**

2 teaspoons **cumin seeds**

2 teaspoons **ground coriander**

2 **red chillies**, deseeded and finely sliced

1 tablespoon **ground cumin**

2 tablespoons finely chopped **garlic**

2 tablespoons peeled and finely chopped **root ginger**

salt

Put the lentils in a deep bowl and cover with boiling water. Leave to soak for 1–2 hours, or overnight if time permits.

When ready to cook, transfer to a colander and rinse under cold running water. Drain and put in the slow cooker pot with the measurement boiling water and coconut milk. Add the turmeric, spinach and tomatoes, cover with the lid and cook for 6–8 hours or until the lentils are tender.

Using a balloon whisk, carefully whisk the mixture until fairly smooth. Stir in the chopped coriander.

Heat the ghee or oil in a small frying pan over a high heat. When hot, quickly add the cumin seeds, ground coriander, chillies, ground cumin, garlic and ginger. Stir-fry for 30–40 seconds, then tip the contents of the frying pan into the dhal. Stir to mix well and season with salt. Serve hot with steamed basmati rice.

Preparation time	**15 minutes**
Cooking temperature	**low**
Cooking time	**4¼–6¼ hours**
Serves	**4**
Heat rating	

1 tablespoon **vegetable oil**

1 large **red onion**, finely chopped

2 **garlic cloves**, minced

1 **Scotch bonnet chilli**, deseeded and finely chopped

2 teaspoons peeled and finely grated **root ginger**

4 **tomatoes**, roughly chopped

275 g (9 oz) **easy-cook basmati rice**

2 **yellow peppers**, halved lengthways, deseeded and thickly sliced

2 **red peppers**, halved lengthways, deseeded and thickly sliced

200 g (7 oz) **okra**, cut into 2 cm (¾ inch) pieces

500 ml (17 fl oz) **boiling water**

small bunch of **coriander**, roughly chopped

Vegetable jollof rice

Heat the oil in a heavy saucepan over a medium heat. Add the onion, garlic, chilli and ginger, and gently fry for about 5 minutes until the onion is soft and translucent.

Transfer this mixture to the slow cooker pot. Tip in the tomatoes, rice, peppers and okra. Pour over the measurement boiling water, cover with the lid and cook for 4–6 hours or until all the liquid is absorbed and the rice and vegetables are tender.

Fluff up the rice grains with a fork, scatter over the coriander and serve in warm bowls or plates.

Preparation time	**10 minutes, plus soaking**
Cooking temperature	**low**
Cooking time	**4¼–6¼ hours**
Serves	**4**
Heat rating	

Green bean & carrot pilaf

Wash the rice in several changes of cold water, then drain. Put in a bowl, cover with fresh cold water and leave to soak for 30 minutes. Drain again and transfer to the slow cooker pot.

Heat the ghee in a heavy pan over a medium-high heat. When it's hot, add the mustard seeds. As soon as they begin to pop (after a matter of seconds), add the chilli, carrots, green beans, turmeric, garam masala and ginger, and stir-fry for 1 minute.

Add this mixture to the rice, stir to mix well and season with salt. Stir in the measurement boiling water, cover with the lid and cook for 4–6 hours or until the liquid is absorbed and the rice is tender. Fluff up the rice grains with a fork and serve immediately.

275 g (9 oz) **easy-cook basmati rice**

3 tablespoons **ghee**

2 teaspoons **mustard seeds**

1 **red chilli**, finely chopped

2 large **carrots**, cut into small dice

100 g (3½ oz) **green beans**, cut into small bite-sized pieces

1 teaspoon **ground turmeric**

1 teaspoon **garam masala**

1 tablespoon peeled and finely grated **root ginger**

600 ml (1 pint) **boiling water**

salt

Preparation time	**10 minutes**
Cooking temperature	**low**
Cooking time	**4¼–6¼ hours**
Serves	**4**
Heat rating	

2 tablespoons **sunflower oil**

1 **onion**, finely chopped

5 cm (2 inch) piece of **cinnamon stick** or **cassia bark**

2 **dried bay leaves**

4 **garlic cloves**, minced

2 teaspoons peeled and finely grated **root ginger**

1 teaspoon **ground coriander**

2 teaspoons **ground cumin**

2 tablespoons mild or **medium curry powder**

400 g (13 oz) **tinned chopped tomatoes**

875 g (1¾ lb) **tinned red kidney beans**, drained

200 ml (7 fl oz) **boiling water**

whisked **natural yogurt**

chopped **coriander leaves**

salt and **pepper**

Spiced red kidney bean curry

Heat the oil in a large heavy saucepan over a medium heat. Add the onion, cinnamon or cassia bark, bay leaves, garlic and ginger, and stir-fry for 4–5 minutes. Stir in the ground coriander, cumin and curry powder, and stir to mix well.

Add the tomatoes and red kidney beans to the slow cooker pot. Stir in the onion mixture and pour over the measurement boiling water. Cover with the lid and cook for 4–6 hours or until the mixture is thick and saucy.

Check the seasoning, adding salt and pepper as needed. Swirl in the whisked yogurt and some chopped coriander just before serving.

Preparation time	10 minutes
Cooking temperature	low
Cooking time	4–6 hours
Serves	4
Heat rating	🌶

Sticky jasmine rice

Put the rice in a sieve and rinse thoroughly under cold running water. Tip the drained rice into the slow cooker pot and add the star anise, black peppercorns, garlic and cinnamon. Pour over the measurement boiling water and stir to mix well. Cover with the lid and cook for 4–6 hours or until the rice is cooked.

Discard the garlic, star anise and cinnamon. Fluff up the grains with a fork, season well with salt and pepper, and serve hot with any curry dish.

250 g (8 oz) **jasmine rice**

3 **star anise**

6 **whole black peppercorns**

2 **garlic cloves**, peeled but left whole

1 **cinnamon stick**

600 ml (1 pint) **boiling water**

salt and **pepper**

Preparation time	10 minutes, plus soaking
Cooking temperature	low
Cooking time	6¼–8¼ hours
Serves	4
Heat rating	🌶🌶

Saag dhal

200 g (7 oz) **yellow split peas**, picked over, rinsed and drained thoroughly

750 ml (1¼ pints) **boiling water**

1 teaspoon **ground turmeric**

100 g (3½ oz) **baby leaf spinach**, roughly chopped

12–15 **cherry tomatoes**

small handful of finely chopped **coriander leaves**

2 tablespoons **ghee** or **vegetable oil**

2 teaspoons **cumin seeds**

2 teaspoons **black mustard seeds**

2 **green chillies**, deseeded and finely sliced

1 tablespoon **ground coriander**

1 tablespoon **ground cumin**

2 tablespoons finely chopped **garlic**

2 tablespoons peeled and finely chopped **root ginger**

salt

Put the split peas in a deep bowl and cover with boiling water. Leave to soak for 1—2 hours or overnight if time permits.

When ready to cook, transfer to a colander and rinse under cold running water. Drain and put in the slow cooker pot with the measurement boiling water. Add the turmeric, spinach and cherry tomatoes. Cover with the lid. Cook for 6—8 hours or until the lentils are tender.

Using a balloon whisk, carefully whisk the mixture until fairly smooth. Stir in the chopped coriander.

Heat the ghee or oil in a small frying pan over a high heat. When hot, quickly add the cumin seeds, mustard seeds, chillies, ground coriander, cumin, garlic and ginger. Stir-fry for 30—40 seconds, then tip the contents of the frying pan into the dhal. Stir to mix well and season with salt.

Serve hot with steamed basmati rice or warm Indian breads such as naans or chapatis.

Preparation time	**5 minutes, plus soaking**
Cooking temperature	**low**
Cooking time	**4¼–6¼ hours**
Serves	**4**
Heat rating	

250 g (8 oz) **basmati rice**

2 tablespoons **sunflower oil**

500 ml (17 fl oz) **boiling water**

400 g (13 oz) **tinned chickpeas**, drained

4 tablespoons chopped **chives**

4 tablespoons chopped **dill**

salt and **pepper**

Herbed rice with chickpeas

Wash the rice in several changes of cold water, then leave to soak in a bowl of fresh cold water for 15 minutes. Drain thoroughly.

Heat the oil in a heavy saucepan over a medium heat and add the drained rice. Cook, stirring, for 30 seconds until the grains are well coated, then add the measurement boiling water and chickpeas. Season well with salt and pepper. Stir to mix well.

Transfer the mixture to the slow cooker pot. Cover with the lid and cook for 4–6 hours or until the liquid is absorbed and the rice is tender.

Fluff up the rice grains with a fork and stir in the chopped herbs. Serve warm with grilled meat, fish or chicken.

Preparation time	**10 minutes**
Cooking temperature	**low**
Cooking time	**4¼–6¼ hours**
Serves	**4**
Heat rating	

Lemon rice

Heat the oil in a nonstick saucepan over a medium heat. Add the curry leaves, chilli, cassia or cinnamon, cloves, cardamom, cumin seeds and turmeric, and stir-fry for 20–30 seconds. Add the drained rice and stir-fry for 2 minutes until the grains are well coated.

Transfer to the slow cooker pot. Add the lemon juice and the measurement boiling water and season well with salt and pepper. Cover with the lid and cook for 4–6 hours or until the liquid is absorbed and the rice is tender.

Fluff up the rice grains with a fork and check the seasoning. Garnish with some chopped coriander and serve hot.

1 tablespoon **sunflower oil**

12–14 **curry leaves**

1 **dried red chilli**

2 **cassia bark** or **cinnamon sticks**

2 or 3 **whole cloves**

4–6 **green cardamom pods**, crushed

2 teaspoons **cumin seeds**

¼ teaspoon **ground turmeric**

225 g (7½ oz) **easy-cook basmati rice**, rinsed and well drained

juice of 1 large **lemon**

500 ml (17 fl oz) **boiling water**

salt and **pepper**

chopped **coriander leaves**, to garnish

Preparation time	**5 minutes**
Cooking temperature	**low**
Cooking time	**4–6 hours**
Serves	4
Heat rating	🌶

275 g (9 oz) **easy-cook long-grain rice**

3 tablespoons **butter**

300 g (10 oz) **green beans,** trimmed and cut into bite-sized lengths

600 ml (1 pint) **boiling chicken stock**

8–10 tablespoons finely chopped **dill**

salt and **pepper**

Middle Eastern dill pilaf

Put the rice, butter and beans in the slow cooker pot. Pour over the boiling stock and season well with salt and pepper. Cover with the lid and cook for 4–6 hours or until the rice is cooked through and the liquid is absorbed.

Fluff up the rice grains with a fork and sprinkle in the dill. Stir to mix well and serve immediately.

Preparation time	20 minutes, plus soaking
Cooking temperature	low
Cooking time	4¼–6¼ hours
Serves	4
Heat rating	🌶

Tomato & coriander rice

275 g (9 oz) **basmati rice**

3 tablespoons **sunflower oil**

4 **shallots**, finely chopped

2 **garlic cloves**, finely chopped

2 teaspoons **cumin seeds**

4 ripe **tomatoes**, skinned, deseeded and finely chopped

500 ml (17 fl oz) **boiling water**

2 tablespoons finely chopped **coriander leaves**

salt and **pepper**

Wash the rice in several changes of cold water, drain and leave to soak in a bowl of cold water for 20–30 minutes. Drain thoroughly and set aside.

Heat the oil in a heavy saucepan over a medium heat and fry the shallots, garlic and cumin seeds for 4–5 minutes until soft and fragrant. Add the tomatoes and drained rice, and stir-fry for 2–3 minutes.

Transfer this mixture to the slow cooker pot. Season well with salt and pepper and pour over the measurement boiling water. Cover with the lid and cook for 4–6 hours or until the liquid is absorbed and the rice is tender.

Fluff up the rice grains with a fork, stir in the chopped coriander and serve immediately.

Preparation time	**15 minutes**
Cooking temperature	**low**
Cooking time	**4½–6½ hours**
Serves	**4**
Heat rating	

Kitcheree

125 g (4 oz) **split red lentils**, picked over, rinsed and thoroughly drained

225 g (7½ oz) **easy-cook basmati rice**, well rinsed and drained

3 tablespoons **sunflower oil**

1 **onion**, finely chopped

1 teaspoon **ground turmeric**

1 tablespoon **cumin seeds**

1 **dried red chilli**

1 **cinnamon stick**

3 **whole cloves**

½ teaspoon **crushed cardamom seeds**

600 ml (1 pint) **boiling vegetable stock**

6 tablespoons finely chopped **coriander leaves**

salt and **pepper**

TO SERVE

assortment of **pickles**

freshly cooked **poppadums**

natural yogurt

Boil the lentils and rice in a large saucepan for 10–12 minutes, then drain thoroughly.

Heat the oil in a heavy saucepan over a medium heat, add the onion and stir-fry for 6–8 minutes until very soft. Add the spices and stir-fry for 2–3 minutes until fragrant. Add the lentil and rice mixture and stir-fry for a further 2–3 minutes.

Transfer this mixture to the slow cooker pot. Pour over the stock and add the coriander. Season well with salt and pepper, cover with the lid and cook for 4–6 hours or until all the liquid is absorbed and the rice is tender.

Serve immediately with the pickles, poppadums and yogurt.

Preparation time	**10 minutes**
Cooking temperature	**low**
Cooking time	**4¼–6¼ hours**
Serves	4
Heat rating	🌶

250 g (8 oz) **easy-cook basmati rice**

300 g (10 oz) **podded broad beans**

50 g (2 oz) **butter**

6 **spring onions**, finely sliced

1 tablespoon **roasted cumin seeds**

500 ml (17 fl oz) **water**

6 tablespoons finely chopped **dill**

salt and **pepper**

small handful of **pomegranate seeds**, to garnish

Broad bean pilaf

Wash the rice in several changes of cold water until the water runs clear.

Meanwhile, cook the broad beans in boiling water for 4–5 minutes. Drain, then put in a bowl of ice-cold water to cool. Remove and discard the skins. Set the beans aside.

Melt the butter in a saucepan over a low heat. Add the spring onions and cumin seeds, and sauté for 2–3 minutes. Add the rice to the pan and stir to coat in the butter.

Transfer this mixture to the slow cooker pot. Cover the rice with the measurement water and season well with salt and pepper. Cover with the lid and cook for 4–6 hours or until the liquid is absorbed and the rice is tender.

Stir the broad beans and dill into the hot rice and scatter with the pomegranate seeds.

Preparation time	10 minutes
Cooking temperature	low
Cooking time	4¼–6¼ hours
Serves	4
Heat rating	🌶

Yellow rice with chickpeas

Heat the oil in a large heavy saucepan over a medium heat. Add the onion and fry for about 5 minutes until soft and translucent. Add the red pepper and garlic and continue frying for a further 2 minutes.

Transfer this mixture into the slow cooker pot. Tip in the rice and stir to mix well. Pour over the measurement boiling water, add the turmeric, chickpeas and beans, and stir to mix well. Cover with the lid and cook for 4–6 hours or until all the liquid is absorbed and the rice and vegetables are tender.

Season with salt and pepper and serve immediately.

2 tablespoons **vegetable oil**

1 **onion**, finely chopped

1 **red pepper**, halved lengthways, deseeded and sliced into strips

1 **garlic clove**, finely chopped

225 g (7½ oz) **basmati rice**

450 ml (¾ pint) **boiling water**

2 teaspoons **ground turmeric**

400 g (13 oz) **tinned chickpeas**, rinsed and drained

100 g (3½ oz) **green beans**

salt and **pepper**

Preparation time	**10 minutes, plus soaking**
Cooking temperature	**low**
Cooking time	**4½–6½ hours**
Serves	**4**
Heat rating	

275 g (9 oz) **easy-cook brown rice**

2 tablespoons **ghee**

2 **onions**, thinly sliced

1 **cinnamon stick**

1 **bay leaf**

6 **whole cloves**

1 **mace blade**

1 teaspoon **sugar**

500 ml (17 fl oz) **boiling water**

salt

Afghani fried brown rice

Soak the rice in a bowl of cold water for 15 minutes. Rinse in a colander, and leave to drain.

Heat the ghee in a heavy saucepan over a medium heat and gently fry the onions for 12–15 minutes until lightly browned and starting to caramelize. Add the cinnamon, bay leaf, cloves and mace and fry for a further 5 minutes. Sprinkle over the sugar, and continue to cook, stirring, for 2–3 minutes until the onion mixture is a rich golden brown.

Transfer the rice into the slow cooker pot and add the onion mixture. Stir to mix well, until the grains are well coated. Season with salt, and pour over the measurement boiling water. Cover with the lid and cook for 4–6 hours or until the rice is cooked through.

Preparation time	10 minutes, plus soaking
Cooking temperature	low
Cooking time	6¼–8¼ hours
Serves	4
Heat rating	🌶🌶🌶

Red lentil curry with tamarind

Place the drained lentils in a bowl and cover with boiling water. Allow to soak for 1 hour, then drain thoroughly.

Put the lentils and turmeric in the slow cooker pot and pour over the measurement boiling water. Cover with the lid and cook for 6–8 hours or until the lentils are tender. When the lentils are cooked, whisk with an electric whisk until fairly smooth.

Heat the oil in a large frying pan over a medium-high heat. When the oil is hot, add the mustard seeds. As soon as they begin to pop, add the curry powder, chillies and bay leaf. Stir-fry for 5–6 seconds until the chillies darken in colour.

Stir in the cooked lentils mixture and season with salt. Add the tamarind paste and palm sugar, and mix well.

250 g (8 oz) **dried red lentils**, picked over and rinsed well

1 teaspoon **ground turmeric**

875 ml (1¼ pints) **boiling water**

2 tablespoons **vegetable oil**

1 teaspoon **black mustard seeds**

1 tablespoon **curry powder**

4 **hot dried red chillies**

1 **bay leaf**

2 teaspoons **tamarind paste**

1 tablespoon **palm sugar**

salt

Preparation time	**15 minutes**
Cooking temperature	**low**
Cooking time	**6½–8½ hours**
Serves	**4–6**
Heat rating	

Mauritian pilaf

4 tablespoons **vegetable oil**

300 g (10 oz) **beef**, such as sirloin or fillet, cut into small bite-sized pieces

300 g (10 oz) **skinless chicken breast** or **thigh fillet**, cut into small bite-sized pieces

1 **onion**, chopped

1 teaspoon **minced garlic**

1 teaspoon peeled and finely grated **root ginger**

1 tablespoon **ground turmeric**

4 **curry leaves**

2 tablespoons finely chopped **coriander leaves**

2 tablespoons chopped **thyme leaves**

3 **whole cloves**

1 teaspoon **whole black peppercorns**

250 g (8 oz) **easy-cook basmati rice**

500 ml (17 fl oz) **boiling water**

salt

Heat the oil in a wide saucepan over a medium-low heat. Sauté the beef and chicken for 6–8 minutes until golden brown. Remove with a slotted spoon and set aside.

Using the same saucepan, sauté the onion, garlic and ginger for 8–10 minutes until the onion is soft and translucent.

Return the beef and chicken to the pan, and add the turmeric, curry leaves, coriander, thyme, cloves and black peppercorns. Stir everything together until well mixed, then add the rice to the pan and cook, stirring, for a further 2–3 minutes until the grains are well coated.

Transfer to the slow cooker pot. Pour over the measurement boiling water and season well with salt. Cover with the lid and cook for 6–8 hours or until the meat is tender and the rice is cooked.

Fluff up the rice grains with a fork and serve immediately.

Preparation time	10 minutes, plus soaking
Cooking temperature	low
Cooking time	6¼–8¼ hours
Serves	4
Heat rating	

250 g (8 oz) **dried red lentils (masoor)**, picked over and rinsed well

1 teaspoon **ground turmeric**

750 ml (1¼ pints) **boiling water**

2 tablespoons **vegetable oil**

2 teaspoons **cumin seeds**

1 teaspoon **crushed coriander seeds**

1 teaspoon **black mustard seeds**

2 tablespoons **curry powder**

2 **green chillies**, finely sliced

10 **curry leaves**

4 **garlic cloves**, finely chopped

1 teaspoon finely chopped **root ginger**

salt

Masoor dhal

Place the drained lentils in a bowl and cover with boiling water. Allow to soak for 1 hour, then drain thoroughly.

Put the lentils and turmeric in the slow cooker pot and pour over the measurement boiling water. Cover with the lid and cook for 6–8 hours or until the lentils are tender. When the lentils are cooked, whisk with an electric whisk until fairly smooth.

Heat the oil in a large, wide frying pan or wok over a medium-high heat. When the oil is hot, add the cumin seeds, coriander seeds, black mustard seeds, curry powder, green chillies, curry leaves, garlic and ginger, and stir-fry for 10–20 seconds.

Add the cooked lentils mixture and season with salt. Stir to mix through. Serve hot with rice and pickles.

Preparation time	5 minutes, plus soaking
Cooking temperature	low
Cooking time	4¼–6¼ hours
Serves	4
Heat rating	🌶

Carrot & pea pilaf

Soak the rice in a bowl of cold water for 20–30 minutes, then drain thoroughly.

Heat the oil in a heavy saucepan over a medium heat. Add the cinnamon, cumin seeds, cloves, cardamom and black peppercorns, and stir-fry for 2–3 minutes until fragrant. Add the carrot and peas, and stir-fry for a further 2–3 minutes.

Transfer this mixture to the slow cooker pot. Tip in the drained rice and stir through. Pour over the measurement boiling water and season well with salt and pepper. Cover with the lid and cook for 4–6 hours or until the liquid is absorbed and the rice is tender.

Fluff up the rice grains with a fork and serve immediately. (To make a quick main course, just toss through some cooked chicken pieces or prawns once the rice is cooked.)

275 g (9 oz) **easy-cook basmati rice**

4 tablespoons **sunflower oil**

1 stick of **cinnamon**

2 teaspoons **cumin seeds**

2 **whole cloves**

4 **green cardamom pods**, lightly bruised

8 **whole black peppercorns**

1 large **carrot**, coarsely grated

200 g (7 oz) **frozen peas**

500 ml (17 fl oz) **boiling water**

salt and **pepper**

Preparation time	**15 minutes**
Cooking temperature	**low**
Cooking time	**4½–6½ hours**
Serves	**4**
Heat rating	

Vegetable biryani

250 g (8 oz) **basmati rice**

6–8 **green cardamom pods**, lightly bruised using a mortar and pestle

750 ml (1¼ pints) **cold water**

large pinch of **saffron threads**

50 g (2 oz) **flaked almonds**

75 ml (3 fl oz) **ghee** or **vegetable oil**

1 large **onion**, thinly sliced

1 medium **cauliflower**, broken into small florets

4 tablespoons **mild curry paste**

200 g (7 oz) **carrots**, peeled and cut into small dice

200 g (7 oz) **fresh** or **frozen peas**

salt

Put the rice and cardamom pods in a large saucepan, and pour over two-thirds of the measurement water. Bring to the boil, then reduce the heat to low. Cover the pan tightly and cook gently for about 8 minutes until the rice is almost tender and the water has been absorbed. Crumble the saffron into the rice, stir through lightly and transfer to the slow cooker pot.

Scatter the almonds into a large frying pan over a low heat and lightly toast for a couple of minutes, being careful not to scorch. Tip into a bowl and set aside.

Heat the ghee or oil in the pan and gently fry the onion and cauliflower for 5 minutes, stirring frequently, until just starting to colour. Add the curry paste, half the toasted almonds and the remaining water. Cook gently, covered, for about 10 minutes, until most of the juices have evaporated.

Tip the vegetable mixture into the rice in the slow cooker pot, and add the carrots, peas and a sprinkling of salt. Stir lightly to mix. Cover with the lid and cook for 4–6 hours or until all the liquid is absorbed and the rice is fluffy and tender.

Scatter with the remaining toasted almonds and serve immediately.

Preparation time	**40 minutes, plus soaking**
Cooking temperature	**low**
Cooking time	**6½–8½ hours**
Serves	**4**
Heat rating	

Dhal makhani

125 g (4 oz) **dried whole black lentils**, picked over, rinsed and drained thoroughly

1 litre (1¾ pints) **boiling water**

3 tablespoons **butter**

1 **onion**, finely chopped

3 **garlic cloves**, crushed

2 teaspoons peeled and finely grated **root ginger**

1 **green chilli**, split in half lengthways

2 teaspoons **cumin seeds**

1 teaspoon **ground coriander**

1 teaspoon **ground turmeric**

1 teaspoon **paprika**, plus extra for sprinkling

200 g (7 oz) **cooked red kidney beans**

large handful of chopped **coriander leaves**

50 ml (2 fl oz) **single cream**

salt

Put the lentils in a deep bowl and cover with cold water. Leave to soak for 10–12 hours. Transfer to a colander and rinse under cold running water. Drain and put in a saucepan with half the measurement boiling water. Bring to the boil and cook for 20 minutes. Drain and set aside.

Melt the butter in a large saucepan over a medium heat. Add the onion, garlic, chilli, cumin seeds and ground coriander, and stir-fry for 5–6 minutes until the onion is soft and translucent. Add the turmeric, paprika, red kidney beans and reserved lentils, and stir through for a minute or so.

Transfer this mixture to the slow cooker pot and pour over the remaining boiling water, cover with the lid and cook for 6–8 hours or until the mixture is thick and saucy and the lentils are tender.

Season with salt, stir in the chopped coriander and drizzle over the cream. Sprinkle over a little extra paprika and serve immediately with rice or warm naan bread.

Preparation time	**10 minutes, plus soaking**
Cooking temperature	**low**
Cooking time	**6¼–8¼ hours**
Serves	**4**
Heat rating	

50 g (2 oz) **yellow split peas**, rinsed and drained

2 tablespoons **vegetable oil**

1 large **onion**, finely chopped

2 large **carrots**, diced

2 medium **potatoes**, peeled and diced

50 g (2 oz) **easy-cook basmati rice**

125 g (4 oz) **lamb fillet**, diced

2 tablespoons **mild curry paste**

900 ml (1½ pints) **boiling water**

small bunch of **coriander**, chopped, plus extra leaves to garnish

salt and **pepper**

Mulligatawny soup

Place the split peas in a bowl and cover with boiling water. Allow to soak for 1 hour, then drain.

Heat the oil in a large saucepan over a medium heat. Add the onion and fry for 3–4 minutes until softened. Add the carrots, potatoes, rice and lamb, and cook for a further 1 minute.

Transfer this mixture to the slow cooker pot. Stir in the split peas and curry paste, then pour in the measurement boiling water and mix well. Season with salt and pepper. Cover with the lid and cook for 6–8 hours or until the vegetables, split peas, meat and rice are tender.

Stir in the coriander, garnish with a few coriander leaves and serve immediately in warm bowls.

Preparation time	15 minutes, plus soaking
Cooking temperature	low
Cooking time	6¼–8¼ hours
Serves	4
Heat rating	

Sri Lankan coconut dhal

250 g (8 oz) **dried red lentils**, picked over and rinsed

2 **shallots**, finely chopped

400 ml (14 fl oz) **coconut milk**

2 ripe **tomatoes**, chopped

2 **green chillies**, sliced

1 teaspoon **ground turmeric**

300 ml (½ pint) **boiling water**

4 tablespoons **vegetable oil**

1 **onion**, finely sliced

8–10 **curry leaves**

2 teaspoons **black mustard seeds**

salt and **pepper**

Place the lentils in a bowl and pour over boiling water to cover. Allow to soak for 1 hour, then drain thoroughly.

Put the lentils, shallots, coconut milk, tomatoes, chillies and turmeric in the slow cooker pot. Add the measurement boiling water and season with salt and pepper. Cover with the lid and cook for 6–8 hours or until the lentils are tender. Whisk the mixture with a balloon whisk until fairly smooth.

Heat the oil in a large frying pan over a medium heat. Add the onion and fry for 6–8 minutes until lightly browned. Add the curry leaves and mustard seeds, and stir-fry for 1–2 minutes until fragrant. Pour the spiced oil mixture over the lentils. Mix well, and serve with rice or flat bread.

Preparation time	**20 minutes, plus marinating**
Cooking temperature	**low**
Cooking time	**7¼–9¼ hours**
Serves	**4**
Heat rating	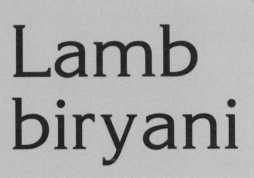

Lamb biryani

500 g (1 lb) boned **leg of lamb**, cut into bite-sized pieces

4 **garlic cloves**, minced

1 teaspoon peeled and finely grated **root ginger**

150 ml (¼ pint) **natural yogurt**

6 tablespoons finely chopped **coriander leaves**

4 tablespoons **sunflower oil**

1 **onion**, finely chopped

1 tablespoon **ground coriander**

1 teaspoon **ground cumin**

1 teaspoon **chilli powder**

1 teaspoon **ground turmeric**

225 g (7½ oz) **tinned chopped tomatoes**

1 teaspoon **saffron threads**

3 tablespoons **warm milk**

400 ml (14 fl oz) **boiling water**

salt and **pepper**

FOR THE RICE

4 tablespoons **sunflower oil**

1 **onion**, halved and thinly sliced

2 teaspoons **cumin seeds**

6 **whole cloves**

10 **whole black peppercorns**

4 **green cardamom pods**

1 **cinnamon stick**

225 g (7½ oz) **easy-cook basmati rice**

Put the lamb in a glass or ceramic dish. Mix together the garlic, ginger, yogurt and coriander, and rub this mixture into the lamb. Cover and marinate in the refrigerator for 4–6 hours.

Heat the oil in a heavy pan over a medium heat, add the onion and fry gently for 12–15 minutes until lightly golden. Add the marinated meat and cook over a high heat for 15 minutes, stirring often, until the meat is well sealed and browned.

Stir in the ground spices and tomatoes, season well with salt and pepper, and bring to the boil. Reduce the heat to low and simmer gently for 30 minutes or until the lamb is tender and most of the liquid has been absorbed. Set aside.

Mix together the saffron and warm milk and set aside.

Meanwhile, heat the oil for the rice in a separate pan over a medium heat. Add the onion, cumin and other spices, and stir-fry for 6–8 minutes. Stir in the rice and stir-fry for a further 2 minutes until the grains are well coated.

Lightly butter the base of the slow cooker pot. Spread a thin layer of the lamb mixture over the bottom and cover evenly with half the rice. Drizzle over half the saffron mixture. Top evenly with the remaining lamb mixture and cover with the remaining rice. Drizzle over the saffron mixture and pour over the measurement boiling water. Cover with the lid and cook for 6–8 hours or until the meat and rice are tender.

Preparation time	**10 minutes, plus soaking**
Cooking temperature	**low**
Cooking time	**4–6 hours**
Serves	**4**
Heat rating	

250 g (8 oz) **easy-cook basmati rice**

4 ripe **tomatoes**, quartered

1 **chicken** or **vegetable stock cube**

1 **cinnamon stick**

2 teaspoons **sugar**

75 g (3 oz) **butter**

salt and **pepper**

Turkish tomato pilaf

Put the rice in a bowl, cover with cold water and stir well. Leave to soak for 30 minutes, then drain in a colander and rinse under cold running water. Drain again thoroughly.

Put the tomatoes in a food processor and blend until liquidized. Measure the resulting tomato juice and add just enough water to make it up to 500 ml (17 fl oz).

Pour the tomato mixture into the slow cooker pot, crumble in the stock cube and add the cinnamon stick and sugar. Season with a little salt and pepper. Tip in the rice and stir well. Cover with the lid and cook for 4–6 hours or until the rice is tender and the liquid has been absorbed.

Stir in the butter and serve immediately with grilled kebabs, meat, fish or chicken.

Preparation time	15 minutes
Cooking temperature	low
Cooking time	4–6 hours
Serves	4
Heat rating	🌶

Vietnamese chicken rice

Put the rice in the slow cooker pot with the chicken, shallots, garlic and ginger, and stir in the chicken stock. Cover with the lid and cook for 6–8 hours or until the liquid is absorbed and the chicken and rice are tender.

Spoon the rice into bowls or onto a serving dish and garnish with the mint and spring onions.

250 g (8 oz) **easy-cook long-grain rice**

500 g (1 lb) boneless **chicken thighs**, skinned and cut into small dice

4 **shallots**, halved and finely sliced

4 **garlic cloves**, finely chopped

1 teaspoon finely chopped **root ginger**

500 ml (17 fl oz) **boiling chicken stock**

TO GARNISH
small bunch of **mint**, leaves picked and finely shredded

4 **spring onions**, finely sliced

Preparation time	**15 minutes, plus soaking**
Cooking temperature	**low**
Cooking time	**4¼–6¼ hours**
Serves	**4**
Heat rating	

Persian pilaf with sour cherries

250 g (8 oz) **easy-cook basmati rice**

200 g (7 oz) **dried sour cherries**

1 teaspoon **saffron threads**

1 tablespoon **hot water**

3 teaspoons **ground cinnamon**

3 tablespoons **vegetable oil**

75 g (3 oz) **butter**, melted

200 ml (7 fl oz) **boiling water**

100 g (3½ oz) **pistachio nuts**, roughly chopped

Wash the rice in a bowl of warm water, then rinse in a sieve under cold running water. Drain thoroughly.

Cover the cherries with cold water and leave to soak for 20 minutes.

Bring a medium-heavy saucepan of salted water to the boil and add the drained rice. Cook for 10–12 minutes until the rice is almost cooked, but retains a little bite. Drain and set aside. Rinse out the saucepan.

Mix the saffron with the measurement hot water, ground cinnamon and oil. Heat 2 tablespoons of the melted butter in the rinsed-out saucepan and stir in the saffron and its soaking liquid, then combine with a ladleful of rice.

Spread this mixture over the bottom of the slow cooker pot, then continue to alternate layers of rice and drained cherries, finishing with a layer of rice on top. Pour over the remaining melted butter and the measurement boiling water. Cover with the lid and cook for 4–6 hours or until the liquid is absorbed and the rice is tender.

Invert onto a platter and serve garnished with the chopped pistachio nuts.

Preparation time	**10 minutes**
Cooking temperature	**low**
Cooking time	**4¼–6¼ hours**
Serves	**4**
Heat rating	

Aromatic prawn pilaf

2 tablespoons **vegetable oil**

1 large **onion,** finely chopped

2 **garlic cloves,** finely chopped

1 tablespoon **curry powder**

250 g (8 oz) **easy–cook basmati rice**

500 ml (1 pint) **boiling water**

finely grated zest and juice of 1 large **lime**

20 g (¾ oz) **coriander,** finely chopped

300 g (10 oz) peeled and deveined **cooked prawns**

salt and **pepper**

Heat the oil in a heavy saucepan over a medium heat. Add the onion and gently fry for 4–5 minutes. Stir in the garlic and curry powder and stir-fry for 1–2 minutes until fragrant, then add the rice and mix well.

Transfer this mixture to the slow cooker pot. Pour in the measurement water and add the lime zest. Season well with salt and pepper, cover with the lid and cook for 4–6 hours or until the stock has been absorbed and the rice is cooked.

Stir in the lime juice, coriander and prawns. Allow the prawns to warm through and serve immediately.

Accompaniments

Preparation time	20 minutes
Cooking temperature	low
Cooking time	6¼–8¼ hours
Makes	about 500 ml (17 fl oz)
Heat rating	

1 tablespoon **sunflower oil**

1 teaspoon peeled and finely grated **root ginger**

2 **garlic cloves**, crushed

5 **whole cloves**

1 **star anise**

2 **cassia bark** or **cinnamon sticks**

5 **whole black peppercorns**

1–2 tablespoons **nigella seeds**

1/2 teaspoon **chilli powder**

875 g (1¾ lb) ripe but firm **mango flesh**, roughly chopped

400 ml (14 fl oz) **white wine vinegar**

275 g (9 oz) **caster sugar**

salt

Sweet mango chutney

Heat the oil in a medium saucepan over a medium heat. Add the ginger, garlic, cloves, star anise, cassia or cinnamon, black peppercorns, nigella seeds and chilli powder, and stir-fry for 1–2 minutes until fragrant. Add the mango, vinegar and sugar. Bring to the boil, stirring gently, until the sugar has dissolved.

Transfer this mixture to the slow cooker pot. Cover with the lid and cook for 6–8 hours or until the mixture is jamlike.

Season with salt and pour into hot sterilized jars. Seal with vinegar-proof lids and allow to cool on a wire rack before storing in the refrigerator. This chutney will keep for 2–3 weeks.

Serve with any Indian curry and rice.

Preparation time	**10 minutes**
Cooking temperature	**low**
Cooking time	**6¼–8¼ hours**
Makes	**about 750 ml (1 ¼ pints)**
Heat rating	

Apple & mango chutney

Heat the oil in a large saucepan over a medium heat. Add the onion and fry for a few minutes until starting to soften. Stir in the ginger and cook, stirring frequently, for 8–10 minutes until the onion is golden. Stir in all of the spices except the turmeric and stir-fry for 1–2 minutes.

Transfer this mixture to the slow cooker pot. Stir in the turmeric, apple, mango, chilli, vinegar and sugar. Pour in the measurement boiling water and season with salt. Cover with the lid and cook for 6–8 hours or until the mixture is thick.

Spoon into hot sterilized jars, cover with vinegar-proof seals and leave to cool on a wire rack. Store in a cool, dark place for 1 week before using and refrigerate once opened. It will keep for up to 1 month.

1 tablespoon **vegetable oil**

1 **onion**, halved and thinly sliced

1 teaspoon peeled and finely grated **root ginger**

1 **cinnamon stick**

¼ teaspoon **cardamom seeds**, crushed

½ teaspoon **coriander seeds**, lightly crushed

¼ teaspoon **nigella seeds**

1 teaspoon **ground turmeric**

1 **cooking apple**, peeled, cored and roughly chopped

400 g (13 oz) **mango flesh**, cut into small bite-sized cubes

1 **red chilli**, finely chopped

150 ml (¼ pint) **white wine vinegar**

150 g (5 oz) **granulated sugar**

200 ml (7 fl oz) **boiling water**

salt

Preparation time	**15 minutes**
Cooking temperature	**high**
Cooking time	**2–3 hours**
Makes	**about 750 ml (1¼ pints)**
Heat rating	🌶🌶🌶

500 g (1 lb) **carrots**, cut into 5 cm (2 inch) batons

200 g (7 oz) small **Thai shallots**, peeled but left whole

6–8 **green chillies**

150 ml (¼ pint) **white wine vinegar**

200 ml (7 fl oz) **water**

½ teaspoon **ground turmeric**

1 teaspoon **salt**

FOR THE PICKLING PASTE

150 ml (¼ pint) **white wine vinegar**

4 **garlic cloves**, minced

2 teaspoons peeled and finely grated **root ginger**

1 tablespoon **black mustard seeds**

2 teaspoons **chilli powder**

1 tablespoon **sugar**

salt

Spiced carrot pickle

Put the carrots, shallots and chillies in the slow cooker pot. Add the vinegar and measurement water, then sprinkle in the turmeric and salt. Cover with the lid and cook for 2–3 hours. Drain the vegetables and set aside.

In a small food processor, blend the vinegar, garlic, ginger, mustard seeds, chilli powder and sugar to a fairly smooth paste. Season with salt, blend again briefly and transfer to a bowl. Add the drained vegetables and toss to coat evenly.

Spoon the pickle mixture into sterilized jars and seal with vinegar-proof lids. Store in a cool, dark place for 2 weeks before eating and refrigerate once opened. It will keep in the refrigerator for up to 1 month.

Serve with any curry and rice.

Preparation time	**10 minutes**
Cooking temperature	**low**
Cooking time	**6¼–8¼ hours**
Serves	**4–6**
Heat rating	♪♪♪

Chilli & tomato chutney

Heat the oil in a frying pan over a medium heat. Add the onion and gently fry for 6–7 minutes until lightly browned. Add the ginger, dried chillies, mustard, cumin and coriander seeds and the garlic. Stir and cook for 2–3 minutes.

Transfer this mixture into the slow cooker pot. Stir in the tomatoes and sugar and season well with salt and pepper. Cover with the lid and cook for 6–8 hours or until thickened.

Pour into hot sterilized jars with tight-fitting lids and leave to cool on a wire rack. Seal well and store in the refrigerator for up to 1 week until ready to use.

Serve at room temperature with any curry and rice dish.

4 tablespoons **vegetable oil**

1 **onion**, halved and thinly sliced

1 teaspoon peeled and finely grated **root ginger**

3 teaspoons **crushed dried red chillies**

2 teaspoons **black mustard seeds**

2 teaspoons **cumin seeds**

1 teaspoon **crushed coriander seeds**

3 **garlic cloves**, thinly sliced

400 g (13 oz) **tinned chopped tomatoes**

200 g (7 oz) **granulated sugar**

salt and **pepper**

Preparation time	10 minutes
Cooking temperature	high
Cooking time	4¼–6¼ hours
Serves	4–6
Heat rating	🌶

1 tablespoon **butter**

1 **onion**, finely chopped

½ **Scotch bonnet chilli**, deseeded and finely chopped

3 large ripe **peaches**, halved, stoned and finely chopped

4 tablespoons **light brown sugar**

6 tablespoons **white wine vinegar**

1 teaspoon **Jamaican jerk seasoning**

100 ml (3½ fl oz) **boiling water**

Jamaican fresh peach chutney

Melt the butter in a small frying pan over a medium heat. Add the onion and chilli and sauté for 5–6 minutes until the onion is soft and translucent.

Transfer this mixture to the slow cooker pot. Add the remaining ingredients and the measurement boiling water and stir to mix well. Cover with the lid and cook for 4–6 hours or until the mixture has thickened slightly.

Serve immediately with any rice dish.

Preparation time	**15 minutes**
Cooking temperature	**low**
Cooking time	**6–8 hours**
Serves	**6–8**
Heat rating	

Indian red cabbage chutney

Put all the ingredients in the slow cooker pot. Cover with the lid and cook for 6–8 hours or until the cabbage is tender and the mixture has thickened.

Spoon the chutney into hot sterilized jars, seal with airtight vinegar-proof lids and cool on a wire rack. Leave to mature in a cool, dark place for about 1 week before using and refrigerate once opened. It will keep for up to 3 weeks in the refrigerator.

Serve with the curry or rice of your choice.

450 g (14½ oz) **red cabbage**, finely shredded

250 g (8 oz) **apples**, peeled, cored and finely chopped

1 tablespoon peeled and finely chopped **root ginger**

3 **garlic cloves**, finely chopped

2 teaspoons **red chilli powder**

1 teaspoon **ground turmeric**

1 **cinnamon stick**

200 g (7 oz) **soft brown sugar**

200 ml (7 fl oz) **red wine vinegar**

Preparation time	**20 minutes**
Cooking temperature	**low**
Cooking time	**6¼–8¼ hours**
Makes	**about 500 ml (17 fl oz)**
Heat rating	

1 tablespoon **sunflower oil**

1 teaspoon peeled and finely grated **root ginger**

5 **whole cloves**

2 tablespoons **coriander seeds**

2 **cassia bark** or **cinnamon sticks**

5 **whole black peppercorns**

1 teaspoon **chilli powder**

875 g (1¾ lb) ripe but firm **pineapple flesh**, roughly chopped

400 ml (14 fl oz) **white wine vinegar**

300 g (10 oz) **golden caster sugar**

salt

Pineapple chutney

Heat the oil in a medium saucepan over a medium heat. Add the ginger, cloves, coriander seeds, cassia or cinnamon, black peppercorns and chilli powder and stir-fry for 1–2 minutes until fragrant. Add the pineapple, vinegar and sugar and bring to the boil, stirring gently until the sugar has dissolved.

Transfer this mixture to the slow cooker pot. Cover with the lid and cook for 6–8 hours or until the mixture is thickened and jamlike.

Season with salt and pour into hot sterilized jars. Seal with vinegar-proof lids and allow to cool on a wire rack before storing in the refrigerator. It will keep for 1–2 weeks.

Serve with any Indian curry and rice.

Preparation time	**10 minutes**
Cooking temperature	**low**
Cooking time	**6–8 hours**
Serves	**4–6**
Heat rating	

Spiced beetroot & apple chutney

Put all the chutney ingredients into the slow cooker pot. Cover with the lid and cook for 6–8 hours or until thickened.

Pour into hot sterilized jars, cover tightly with vinegar-proof lids and leave to cool on a wire rack before storing in the refrigerator. It will keep for up to 2 weeks.

Serve at room temperature with any curry and rice dish.

3 medium **onions**, finely chopped

250 ml (8 fl oz) **white wine vinegar**

500 g (1 lb) cooked (but not vinegared) **beetroot**, finely chopped

2 firm **cooking apples**, peeled, cored and finely chopped

200 g (7 oz) **soft brown sugar**

1 tablespoon **crushed coriander seeds**

1 tablespoon **crushed cumin seeds**

2 teaspoons **salt**

Preparation time	10 minutes
Cooking temperature	low
Cooking time	6¼–8¼ hours
Serves	4–6
Heat rating	

2 large **cucumbers**, halved lengthways and deseeded

125 ml (4 fl oz) **malt vinegar**

200 ml (7 fl oz) **boiling water**

1 teaspoon **salt**

4 tablespoons **groundnut oil**

2 tablespoons **light sesame oil**

8 **garlic cloves**, thinly sliced

1 **onion**, finely sliced

2 tablespoons **sesame seeds**

Burmese cucumber pickle

Cut the cucumber into strips of finger thickness, then cut strips into 5 cm (2 inch) pieces and place in the slow cooker pot. Add the vinegar, measurement boiling water and salt, cover with the lid and cook for 6–8 hours or until the cucumber is translucent. Drain and set aside to cool.

In a frying pan, heat the oils over a medium heat and fry the garlic for 2–3 minutes until pale golden. Remove with a slotted spoon and drain on kitchen paper. Add the onion to the same pan and fry for 6–8 minutes until lightly browned.

Meanwhile, toast the sesame seeds in a separate dry frying pan over a low heat, stirring constantly so they do not scorch.

To serve, mix together the cooled cucumber, the oil from the frying pan, the garlic, onion and sesame seeds.

Preparation time	**20 minutes, plus soaking**
Cooking temperature	**low**
Cooking time	**6½–8½ hours**
Serves	**4–6**
Heat rating	

Lemon & date pickle

Put the dried chillies and mustard seeds in a bowl. Pour over the vinegar and leave to soak for 24 hours.

Transfer the vinegar and chilli mixture to a blender. Add the garlic and ginger and blend until fairly smooth. Put the blended mixture and the sugar in a large non-corrosive saucepan and bring to the boil. Reduce the heat to low and gently simmer for 20–30 minutes until thickened.

Transfer this mixture to the slow cooker pot. Add the dates, lemons and sultanas to the pot, cover with the lid and cook for 6–8 hours or until thickened and jamlike.

Spoon into hot sterilized jars, seal with vinegar-proof lids and leave to cool on a wire rack. Store in a cool, dark place and refrigerate once opened. It will keep for up to 1 month.

10 **dried red chillies,** stalks removed and deseeded

1 tablespoon **black mustard seeds**

500 ml (17 fl oz) **white wine vinegar**

20 **garlic cloves,** roughly chopped

2 tablespoons peeled and finely grated **root ginger**

400 g (13 oz) **caster sugar**

500 g (1 lb) **dried dates,** halved and pitted

6 **preserved** or **pickled lemons,** roughly chopped

200 g (7 oz) **sultanas**

Index

Acknowledgements

Executive Editor Eleanor Maxfield
Editor Ruth Wiseall
Creative Director Tracy Killick
Design Cobalt id
Illustrator Natacha Ledwidge
Production Controller Linda Parry